FACILITATION

Latest titles in the McGraw-Hill Training Series

TRAINING TO MEET THE TECHNOLOGY CHALLENGE
Trevor Bentley   ISBN 0-07-707589-7

IMAGINATIVE EVENTS Volumes I & II
A Sourcebook of Innovative Simulations, Exercises, Puzzles and Games
Ken Jones   ISBN 0-07-707679-6 Volume I
                        ISBN 0-07-707680-X Volume II
                        ISBN 0-07-707681-8 for set of Volumes I & II

LEARNING THROUGH SIMULATIONS
A Guide to the Design and Use of Simulations in Business and Education
John Fripp   ISBN 0-07-707588-9

MEETINGS MANAGEMENT
A Manual of Effective Training Material
Leslie Rae   ISBN 0-07-707782-2

WORKSHOPS THAT WORK
100 Ideas To Make Your Training Events More Effective
Tom Bourner, Vivien Martin
and Phil Race   ISBN 0-07-707800-4

TRAINING FOR PROFIT
A Guide to the Integration of Training In An Organization's Success
Philip Darling   ISBN 0-07-707786-5

THE HANDBOOK FOR ORGANIZATIONAL CHANGE
Strategy and Skill For Trainers and Developers
Carol A. O'Connor   ISBN 0-07-707693-1

MANAGING THE TRAINING PROCESS
Putting the Basics into Practice
Mike Wills   ISBN 0-07-707806-3

DEVELOPING DIRECTORS
Building An Effective Boardroom Team
Colin Coulson-Thomas ISBN 0-07-707590-9

RESOURCE-BASED LEARNING
Using Open and Flexible Resources For Continuous Development
Julie Dorrell   ISBN 0-07-707692-3

Details of these and other titles in the series are available from:

The Product Manager, Professional Books, McGraw-Hill Book Company Europe,
Shoppenhangers Road, Maidenhead, Berkshire SL6 2QL, United Kingdom.
Telephone: 0628 23432. Fax: 0628 770224

Facilitation

Providing opportunities for learning

Trevor Bentley

McGRAW-HILL BOOK COMPANY

London · New York · St Louis · San Francisco · Auckland
Bogotá · Caracas · Lisbon · Madrid · Mexico · Milan
Montreal · New Delhi · Panama · Paris · San Juan · São Paulo
Singapore · Sydney · Tokyo · Toronto

Published by
McGRAW-HILL Book Company Europe
Shoppenhangers Road, Maidenhead, Berkshire SL6 2QL, England.
Telephone: 0628 23432
Fax: 0628 770224

British Library Cataloguing in Publication Data
Bentley, Trevor J.
    Facilitation: Providing Opportunities for Learning. — (McGraw-Hill Training
Series)
    I. Title II. Series
    658.3124

    ISBN 0-07-707684-2

Library of Congress Cataloging-in-Publication Data
Bentley, Trevor J.
    Facilitation: providing opportunities for learning/Trevor
Bentley.
        p.   cm. — (McGraw-Hill training series)
    Includes bibliographical references and index.
    ISBN 0-07-707684-2
    1. Communication in small groups.   2. Group relations training.
    3. Decision-making, Group. I. Title. II. Series.
    HM133.B46   1993
    302.3'4—dc20   93-31420
                                                CIP

12345 CL 97654

Typeset by Book Ens Limited, Baldock, Herts
Printed and bound in Great Britain by Clays Ltd, St Ives plc

To all my friends at BEACON and
Scott, Howard, Marty, Bill and Neil
with whom I shared and learned so much

Contents

Series preface

Training and development are now firmly centre stage in most organizations, if not all. Nothing unusual in that—for some organizations. They have always seen training and development as part of the heart of their businesses—but more and more must see it the same way.

The demographic trends through the 1990s will inject into the marketplace severe competition for good people who will need good training. Young people without conventional qualifications, skilled workers in redundant crafts, people out of work, women wishing to return to work—all will require excellent training to fit them to meet the job demands of the 1990s and beyond.

But excellent training does not spring from what we have done well in the past. T&D specialists are in a new ball game. 'Maintenance' training—training to keep up skill levels to do what we have always done—will be less in demand. Rather, organization, work, and market change training are now much more important and will remain so for some time. Changing organizations and people is no easy task, requiring special skills and expertise which, sadly, many T&D specialists do not possess.

To work as a 'change' specialist requires us to get to centre stage—to the heart of the company's business. This means we have to ask about future goals and strategies, and even be involved in their development, at least as far as T&D policies are concerned.

This demands excellent communication skills, political expertise, negotiating ability, diagnostic skills—indeed, all the skills a good internal consultant requires.

The implications for T&D specialists are considerable. It is not enough merely to be skilled in the basics of training, we must also begin to act like business people and to think in business terms and talk the language of business. We must be able to resource training not just from within but by using the vast array of external resources. We must be able to manage our activities as well as any other manager. We must share in the creation and communication of the company's vision. We must never let the goals of the company out of our sight.

In short, we may have to grow and change with the business. It will be hard. We shall not only have to demonstrate relevance but also value for money and achievement of results. We shall be our own boss, as accountable for results as any other line manager, and we shall have to deal with fewer internal resources.

The challenge is on, as many T&D specialists have demonstrated to me over the past few years. We need to be capable of meeting that challenge. This is why McGraw-Hill Book Company Europe have planned and launched this major new training series—to help us meet that challenge.

The series covers all aspects of T&D and provides the knowledge base from which we can develop plans to meet the challenge. They are practical books for the professional person. They are a starting point for planning our journey to the twenty-first century.

Use them well. Don't just read them. Highlight key ideas, thoughts, action pointers or whatever, and have a go at doing something with them. Through experimentation we evolve; through stagnation we die.

I know that all the authors in the McGraw-Hill Training Series would want me to wish you good luck. Have a great journey into the twenty-first century.

ROGER BENNETT
Series Editor

About the series editor

Roger Bennett has over 20 years' experience in training, management education, research and consulting. He has long been involved with trainer training and trainer effectiveness. He has carried out research into trainer effectiveness, and conducted workshops, seminars, and conferences on the subject around the world. He has written extensively on the subject including the book *Improving Trainer Effectiveness*, Gower. His work has taken him all over the world, and has involved directors of companies as well as managers and trainers.

Roger Bennett has worked in engineering, several business schools (including the International Management Centre, where he launched the UK's first masters degree in T&D), and has been a board director of two companies. He is the editor of the *Journal of European Industrial Training*, and was series editor of the ITD's *Get In There* workbook and video package for the managers of training departments. He now runs his own business called The Management Development Consultancy.

Preface

The young woman looked at me across the circle and said, 'If you think you can manipulate me like this then I am going to disappoint you'. She folded her arms and looked at me defiantly.

'What do you think I am trying to do?', I asked.

'You are trying to get me to cry', she replied.

'Do you want to cry?', I asked.

'No', she answered, but I could see the tears in her eyes.

'What would you like to do next?', I asked her.

'I think it would be good if we moved on', she answered.

'Good—then let's move on', I suggested.

We started the next activity and about half way through I heard someone crying. It was the same young woman.

I don't know how this happened: whether it had anything to do with the way I was facilitating, or just the young woman taking the opportunity to do something she wanted to do. This is the problem about facilitation: there are no clear cut rules about what to do and when to do it. There is, however, a process, and there are some techniques, or strategies, that can be useful.

In this book I am going to share my experiences with you in such a way that the process I follow is explained, and some of the things I do are described. I have learned to facilitate by observing other facilitators and by practising, experimenting, and following my intuition.

This book is then a journey through my experience so far, and as such is perhaps as much an adventure for me to write as it is for you to read.

Although the book might seem to offer ways of dealing with certain types of situation, I must remind you that in facilitation every situation is different, and what worked previously in a similar situation might not work in the current one.

To provide some flow and structure to the book I have divided what I have to say into four parts. To link these together and bring the book to life, I have used a case study based on a real workshop which I ran. The names of the participants have of course been changed.

Part One deals with the process of working with groups. A large part of my work is concerned with facilitating groups in a range of different activities, and with different needs. During this work I have developed certain ways in which I find it possible to enable groups to work well together. This is what I share with you in Part One.

Part Two is my view of the skills needed to facilitate successfully. This is by no means exhaustive, and all facilitators bring their own particular set of personal skills and experience to the task of facilitation.

Part Three I have called 'Intervention strategies', because I believe that the way facilitators intervene in the group process is fundamental to their success. So here I look at those things that I have found useful in the way I intervene. Often I am unsure of what I have done, or how I have done it, but in this part I have tried to set out, mostly by example, the things that I hope you will find interesting and useful.

Part Four is about managing interaction. Perhaps the word 'managing' is too strong a word, but it is the only one I can think of which reflects what I do as a facilitator. Interaction in a group, or between two people, is the main point at which people learn, and change occurs.

It is important to me that such interaction is constructive, even if it appears destructive, this is why I think the process I use is one of management.

Author's warning:

The inappropriate and careless use of the ideas and approaches in this book could seriously damage your wealth and reputation.

I want to encourage you to experiment and take risks, but not at the expense of participants, or your own learning. Practice one new thing at a time until you feel confident to be more adventurous. The difference between very good and very bad facilitation is often only a matter of degree.

As I write this prologue I am sitting in the grounds of a villa in Italy, where I have been spending some time with an international group of gestalt therapists. I am well aware that my ideas about facilitation are mine alone, based on my own experience, but I have been pleased to discover that much of what I do and the way I do it is shared by my colleagues as being relevant, practical, and sufficiently flexible to be worth sharing with you in the form of this book.

I hope that my adventure through my own experience makes enjoyable and useful reading.

TREVOR BENTLEY
Il Colle, Casenove, Italy

Acknowledgements

Substantial extracts within this book were taken from:

Benjamin Hoff, *The Tao of Pooh*, Methuen Children's Books, London. Copyright © Benjamin Hoff 1982.

Kahlil Gibran, *The Prophet*, Mandarin, London. Reproduced by permission of William Heinemann Ltd.

A.A. Milne, *The Pooh Book of Quotations*, Methuen Children's Books, London. Copyright © Michael John Brown, Peter Janson-Smith, R.H.V.C. Morgan and T.M. Robinson (Trustees of The Pooh Properties) 1986.

John Heider, *The Tao of Leadership*, published by Wildwood House, Aldershot. Copyright © Ashgate Publishing Ltd.

Carl Rogers, *Client centred therapy*, Constable Publishers, London. Copyright © 1951 by Houghton Mifflin Company

Carl Rogers, *Freeedom to Learn*, C.E. Merrill, Ohio. Reprinted with the permission of Merrill, an imprint of Macmillan Publishing Company from *Freedom to Learn* by Carl Rogers. Copyright © 1983 by Bell & Howell Company.

F. Perls, R.F. Hefferline and P. Goodman, *Gestalt therapy*, Souvenir Press Ltd., London. Copyright © 1972. Reprinted by permission of Souvenir Press Ltd.

PART ONE

Working with groups

Thirteen people sit in a circle, but it is the climate or the spirit in the centre of the circle, where nothing is happening, that determines the nature of the group field.[1]

When people come together in a group their individual energy merges and forms a group energy. This process starts immediately the group meets, but the merging itself may take a long time. The people in the group have to relate to each other, to the group and to the facilitators.

I find this process of group formation a fascinating process and one that I doubt I will ever fully understand. I think that people give to the group what they want to give, and that they take what they want to take. Facilitators do the same thing, but from a different perspective.

Part One looks at the group process from the facilitator's point of view. If a group was left entirely to itself without a facilitator it would develop its own energy and identity. So I see the role of the facilitator as one of helping the group to form more quickly and more effectively than might otherwise be the case. To create an environment of safety in which people can explore relationships with others in the group.

This part contains five chapters in which I look at how, as a facilitator, I try to help this process of group formation and identity.

References

1. Heider, John (1986) *The Tao of Leadership*, Aldershot: Wildwood House.

1 Establishing roles

Whenever groups meet, the people forming the group tend to arrive with certain assumptions about the roles of the various participants. These assumptions vary depending on the reasons for which the group has gathered.

Discovering what these assumptions are, and the expectations that stem from them, is an important formative process. One approach is for the group to meet and allow the roles of the individuals to emerge as the group interaction proceeds. This is an exciting and illuminating approach, but can for some people be extremely difficult and far too challenging. Another approach is for the facilitator to guide the group through a process of role clarification.

I tend to use three different approaches, depending on the circumstances. I usually wait to decide what to do until the group meets. But sometimes I might decide on an opening approach when I am thinking about working with the group in advance of the first meeting. These three approaches are:

- To allow the group to meet and to interact in an unstructured, non-directed way.
- To encourage the group to explore their individual reasons for being there, and to consider the roles that they expect everyone will play.
- To start by introducing myself and explaining the way I see my role in the group, and what I expect from group members. I follow this by asking the individuals to introduce themselves and say what they think about group roles.

The important aspect of determining roles is to allow the group the space and time to clarify what is expected of them, and what they expect of others. One way to do this is for participants to work in pairs and to share their expectations with their partner. Each person takes a turn and then the pairs return to the main group and share what they discovered about the similarities and differences in their expectations.

This need not necessarily take more than a few minutes, and only happens when the group first meets or if a new member joins the group.

This was the first meeting of the group. Joe, who was assisting me, had previously asked me how we would start. I suggested that we took a completely unstructured approach.

We had arranged a circle of chairs in the library, choosing this pleasant comfortable room rather than one of the Spartan 'lecture' rooms. We were expecting ten participants at this facilitation skills workshop.

It was 6 p.m. on a Sunday evening at the start of a five-day workshop. I arrived in the library to find five people sitting in the prearranged chairs. I said hello and joined them, Joe was already there. People drifted in, and within five minutes the chairs were full. There was some nervous chatter going on. Joe and I sat quietly waiting.

After about three minutes of silence, which was growing heavier and heavier, a rather tense looking man in suit and tie said, 'Well, what are we waiting for?'.

Joe asked him what he thought he was waiting for, and in an irritated way he said, 'I'm waiting for someone to start this workshop'.

'What do you think we should do?', I asked.

'Well, at least we could introduce ourselves', he said.

This suggestion was followed by a lively thirty minutes during which everyone introduced themselves to the group (see Appendix 1 for the introductions).

After the introductions I asked the group what they would like to do next. The same rather 'stiff' man, who we now knew was called Derek, said he would like to know why we were working in the library and not in one of the excellent training rooms. I suggested that perhaps we needed to sort out one or two things, like where we were going to work, when people wanted to start and finish and so on. Derek was looking rather annoyed and anxious.

'Why don't you just tell us and give us the programme?' he stated, in a very challenging way.

I didn't reply, and Joe said that we intended to look at the programme later, and that perhaps we could resolve some of the outstanding issues by discussing in pairs how we wanted the workshop to be to get what we wanted from it. The group were very willing and relieved to receive even this gentle form of direction.

Even at this stage in the group's formation certain roles are beginning to appear. Joe and I can be seen as the facilitators, and we have taken the role of guides. Derek has clearly appointed himself as the person who will question what is happening, in the apparent hope of receiving some direction. It is debatable whether or not we needed to take the role definition further at this stage, unless the group decided they wanted to do so.

It is probable that most people have an idea of what they expect the facilitator to do, and/or be responsible for, in the group. Establishing what this is can be a very useful and informative exercise for a group to carry out. What is almost certain to emerge is that individuals have different expectations, which seem to me to be linked to their personal needs for help, support and protection in the group process.

It is tempting to define the role of the facilitator and to follow this with a list of desirable attributes, but I am not going to give way to this temptation. What I will say is that facilitators have to remember always that whenever a group meets there is a group process that comes into being. This process belongs to the group. It is a combination of the living processes of all the people in the group and has to be respected.

Remember that you are facilitating another person's process. It is not your process. Do not intrude. Do not control. Do not force your own needs and insights into the foreground. If you do not trust a person's process, that person will not trust you.[1]

It is my intention that by the time you have reached the end of the book you will be able to assess for yourself what the skills and attributes are for good facilitation. (You will find an exercise on p. 116–118 to help you do this.) The great problem that I have with defining facilitation in these terms is that what is appropriate, and works in one situation, will fail completely in another. There is no alternative but to concentrate completely on what is happening and to respond as seems most appropriate at the time.

There are moments, especially at the start of a group, when what is happening is stimulated by a suggestion from the facilitator. This is a very useful way to encourage the group to become involved in the group process.

When the group returned from the discussions in pairs I left if for Joe to ask what they wanted to share with the group. There was much animated discussion as the various pairs told us what they had decided was important, and at the suggestion of Margaret a list was prepared on a flip chart that Derek brought into the library from one of the training rooms.

Using the list as a focus the group decided which room we would work in; the times we would start and finish (at least as a guide); what they expected from Joe and me, and what they were prepared to do themselves. When this process seemed to have been completed I asked the group what they wanted to do next. After some discussion, in which Derek and Margaret said the most, it was agreed that we would move into the selected room.

When we did this, the group, under Melanie's leadership, rearranged the chairs in a circle. We sat down and Michael said, 'OK, so what happens now?'.

At this stage in the group formation individual roles and interactions are beginning to appear. This can now be allowed to develop. The exercise has served several purposes. It has given every participant a chance to say what they think about what they need and expect from the facilitators. It has given them an opportunity to start to take responsibility for the things the group does and how the group does them. And it has provided an opportunity for a group process to begin to grow.

If we had chosen to approach the issue of roles by setting out what we believed the roles to be, we would no doubt have generated discussion as participants chose to agree, to disagree, or to say nothing, but we would not have allowed the group process to flow. Our approach would have been more of a block to the group development than an aid.

I can recall a time, not that long ago, when I would have been insisting on spelling out roles carefully so that everyone was clear. But trying to avoid confusion in this way generally serves to prevent group development, and allows little space for contact between participants and between participants and facilitators.

A great deal of what I am going to be saying in this book is about contact, and how good contact can lead to the building of an effective human environment in which people can grow and develop. Perhaps establishing, or at least helping the group to establish, such an environment is the key role of the facilitator.

I never find it easy to make a decision about the clarification of roles, and there can be occasions when there are many roles other than those of facilitator and participant. When this occurs I still believe in encouraging the group to sort out whatever clarity they neeed.

One large group I was a member of, as a participant, had the following roles being played out: facilitator, co-facilitator, assistant facilitator, support group leaders, support group assistants and participants. The support group leaders and assistants were also participants. The usefulness of trying to spell out these individual roles and of doing so in a way that participants would remember and find helpful is highly debatable.

The important aspect of this question for me is whether or not the individuals fulfilling these different roles understand and can explain, if needed, the role they expect to carry out. However, even this is less important than the overriding need for people, whatever their role, to be attentive to and aware of what is happening in the group.

Here are the three key requirements that I always consider I have to meet when I am facilitating a group.

- To provide opportunities for the group to go in the direction that they want, or seem to want, to go in.
- To constantly be aware of what is happening in the group.
- To stay quiet and be attentive to the needs of the individual participants in the group.

By doing these three things I can serve the group and ensure that the energy is focused on group needs.

References

1. Heider, John (1986) *The Tao of Leadership*, Aldershot: Wildwood House.

2 Setting agendas

Participants usually come to a group with their own agenda. They may not have sorted out, or even thought consciously about, exactly what it is, but they will have an agenda. This agenda will include expectations, hopes, issues, fears, objectives and concerns. I feel it is important for participants to set their own agendas, and if they want to, to share this with the group, In this way it is sometimes possible to create a group agenda. Even when this is done there will still be hidden agendas that participants are unwilling or unable to share.

Some years ago I always started my workshops with a discussion of planned learning objectives, asking each participant to list what they wanted and expected to learn. I would follow this with an outline of the workshop, which would hopefully, cover what the participants expected. The topics on my outline programme might even have been allocated time slots during the planned duration of the workshop.

I was aware that this approach felt very comfortable for me and seemed to be appreciated by participants, but it was also relatively passive and uninvolving. Then I started to experiment with a less directive approach, and although I had prepared a list of key topics I did not place them into a timed programme. This was very successful, both in creating more involvement and in promoting the feeling that the workshop was going to cover what participants wanted. Even so, on a couple of occasions I was challenged to reveal my 'hidden' agenda. One participant on a training skills workshop commented, 'You must have a programme. It is impossible to run a workshop without one. You're just not sharing it with us'.

Of course, his comment was accurate. I did have my own idea of the programme we would follow. I had my agenda just as everyone else had theirs.

My next approach, which I am still experimenting with, was to guide the group through an agenda setting process in which I and my co-facilitators play a full part. In this way, my hidden agenda becomes part of the group's agenda in the same way that I am a part of the group.

After Michael's comment about what happens next I stayed quiet. Joe looked around the group but said nothing. After a short time Derek spoke.

'I want to know if anybody else is feeling frustrated by the way we seem to be working'.

Nobody answered, so I asked Derek what was so frustrating for him. 'It's this lack of direction, I want to know what we are going to do next, and I want you to take some control and act as a leader.'

'So you want me to tell you what to do?', I responded.

'Well, not exactly, but you could give us a clue', he said, with a quick smile.

I asked if anyone else would like to say how they were feeling. This was followed by hesitant comments from some people about how uncomfortable the process was, and from others about how tense and involved they felt.

I then responded by saying we had thirty minutes before dinner and that we could spend the time in three groups of four discussing what we would like to see on the agenda for the workshop, and that after dinner we could share our ideas with the group and create an overall agenda. This suggestion was met with relief, and we quickly formed small groups (we used the 1, 2, 3, round the group method for this).

Over dinner (around one large table) there was a high level of social interaction as people continued to find out about other participants and reveal themselves.

Some were more talkative than others, and some of the conversation seemed nervous and hesitant, but the group appeared to be developing an identity already.

When we reassembled I asked the group how long they wanted to work for before we relaxed for what was left of the evening. An hour was agreed. I then asked if someone would volunteer to help the group to formulate an agenda. Michael said he would do it.

For the next 30 minutes each of the small groups shared their ideas with the group and these were listed by Michael. When this was complete Michael suggested that we should group all the items (over 30) into categories, such as interpersonal skills etc. This was agreed, and after another 25 minutes the task was complete.

Michael then asked me if this was OK. I said ask the group, which he did. Bob thought that we could prioritize the items and decide where we wanted to start. This was generally agreed, but Jenny said she was very tired and wanted to do it in the morning. So we finished and headed for the bar.

During the agenda-setting process described above, both Joe and I had contributed our thoughts as part of the small groups, and then as part of the main group. I deliberately asked for a volunteer to lead the feedback session so that the process would be seen as a group process and not as a facilitator-led (manipulated) one.

In following this approach, the facilitator has to bear in mind the overall purpose of the group, but I have used this approach successfully with group meetings as diverse as therapy groups, a board of directors discussing financial strategy, and working together, or team-building, groups.

You may choose to work with a programme which will provide a framework for the group. If you do this I think it is very important to discuss it with the group as part of an agenda-setting exercise. I am always careful when using a programme, which I don't do very often, because I am aware that it sets boundaries and creates expectations around the work we are going to do. And if the programme is timed it generates a continuous time pressure which is never helpful.

When using a programme or a set of predetermined objectives, declare what they are; allow room for change; avoid setting specific times; and avoid facilitating to meet the programme.

No matter what the assumed purpose of the group meeting is, or how long the meeting is scheduled for, I believe that it is vital for the participants to have the opportunity to check out their 'assumed' agendas and for the group to agree on what it wants to achieve.

During the agenda-setting, I tend to encourage participants to make a note of their own specific agenda items as well as contributing to the development of the group agenda. I further suggest that it will be up to them to ensure that their own needs are met. This is sometimes greeted with hostility, especially from people who have been conditioned to a process where the leader is assumed to be responsible for everyone achieving what they want. This is often apparent in training groups, where people are often sent to 'be trained', rather than going to learn out of choice.

For some years I worked with a trainer who was keen on agreeing 'learning contracts' with participants. These would involve participants 'contracting' with the trainer what they expected to achieve and the help they thought they needed from the trainer. This was intended to clarify and objectify the learning process.

I watched this approach in operation and I came to believe that it introduced an unnecessary degree of rigidity in what, I believe, is a highly flexible process. I prefer to explore roles and expectations in a more fluid way and to encourage participants to flow with the learning as it happens.

When we assembled in the morning Derek was wearing a badge with his name and job title on. We had deliberately not issued badges, and I was intrigued, but I didn't mention it. I asked Michael if he would like to finish where we left off last night, and he agreed.

It didn't take long for the group to agree the priorities, although there were some wide differences between what people thought was most important. However, by asking them to highlight and keep a record of their own needs, which I did, we were able to prepare a prioritized list of items for action.

'OK: so we now have an agenda.' It was Derek speaking. 'It has taken us a couple of hours last night and an hour this morning to get here when you could've given us this list when we started. Can you please tell my why?' Derek sat back with a resigned sigh.

The group was quiet and expectant so I asked them to think about what we had done and to discuss their thoughts with the person next to them. I suggested we take five minutes each to do this.

At the end of ten minutes I suggested that we go round the group and ask each person to say what they thought about the way we, as a group, had set our agenda.

The feedback was extensive and varied from 'effective but frustrating' (Jenny and Derek), to 'fascinating and exciting' (Joe, Margaret and Melanie). The remainder were accepting, and a couple of 'accepting but sceptical' (Sid and Michael). The majority of the group had enjoyed the process and were looking forward to the next stage (see Appendix 2 for individual comments).

For me, the biggest advantage of this approach is the development of an attitude in the group that this is their agenda and their workshop. In the past, when I have produced programmes or lists of topics, people have been attending 'my' workshop, and they have not related my programme to their own individual needs. This generates an in-built apathy to what is happening rather than commitment and involvement.

The second, and equally important benefit is the way this process enables the group to work together and take responsibility from the start for what is happening. Nothing could be more important than the group agreeing on their working agenda for the next five days. Not only are they committed to it, they are also looking forward eagerly to dealing with the items on the agenda. In addition, their curiosity is aroused as to how the items will be dealt with.

The third thing that is gained is a sense of freedom for the facilitators to concentrate on the group process rather than to be the source of information, knowledge and wisdom. As a facilitator, I do not see it as my job to answer questions, but rather to help the group discover their own answers. I do, of course, bring my knowledge to the group, and I will share it with the group in the exercises, such as the agenda-setting, when my ideas are built in to the group agenda. I believe that people already know the answers to the questions they ask, but don't have the confidence to trust the answers they already have. If I provide the space and safety for them to explore their own knowledge, then I do far more than if I simply give them my answer to their question.

No man can reveal to you aught but that which already lies half asleep in the dawning of your knowledge. If he is indeed wise he does not bid you enter the house of his wisdom, but rather leads you to the threshold of your own mind.[1]

References

1. Gibran, Kahlil (1991) *The Prophet*, London: Mandarin.

3 Matching needs

Every group is made up of individual people who, though they may contribute to a group agenda, will have their own specific needs that they want met.

I doubt if in any group the facilitator will ever succeed in providing opportunities through which the needs of everyone in the group can be answered, but it is important to try to set up an environment which at least opens up the possibility. Such an environment will depend to a large extent on the clarity with which participants are able to recognize and express their needs.

When the agenda-setting process has been completed, I think that it is useful to pause before working through the agenda to check that everyone is able to identify their specific needs at three levels:

- The support, help, recognition, acceptance etc. they need to work in the group, i.e. themselves.
- How they prefer to learn/deal with the content, i.e. their process.
- The items on the group agenda which they think are particularly relevant to them, i.e. their content.

By getting everybody to focus on themselves in this way it becomes possible for the facilitators and the individuals to take control of their own process. This self-focus also helps everyone to interact with the group to (a) get what they need for themselves, and (b) help others to get what they want. It is through self-focus that co-operative personal development and growth can take place.

Generally speaking, we are not very good at focusing on ourselves. We have been conditioned by parents, teachers and society that self-awareness and self-centredness are the same as selfishness. But I would argue that until we have learned to focus inward and to come to know ourselves it is impossible to be selfless.

The Wise are Who They Are. They work with what they've got and do what they can do. There are things about ourselves that we need to get rid of; there are things we need to change. But at the same time, we do not need to be too desperate, too ruthless, too combative. Along the way to usefulness and happiness, many of those things will change themselves, and the others can be worked on as we go. The first thing we need to do is recognize and trust our own Inner Nature, and not lose sight of it. For within the Ugly Duckling is the Swan, inside the Bouncy Tigger is the Rescuer who knows the Way, and in each of us is something Special and *that* we need to keep.[1]

If this sense of self is so important, and I think it is paramount, then it is worth spending some time with the group to explore ourselves. As a group, we can do this in many ways. The choice depends upon the circumstances, the willingness, and readiness of the group.

I asked the group if they would like to spend some time setting the objectives they would like to achieve during the rest of the workshop. I explained briefly that we would stop from time to time to look at how well we were progressing, and that it might help if they had their own personalized objectives against which they could measure their progress. This suggestion was well received. So I then asked if anyone had any ideas about how we could do this.

After a short time Melanie said that she would like to spend some time on her own just thinking about what she wanted to achieve. The others went along with this so we agreed they would reassemble in the group in 30 minutes time.

Joe and I stayed in the group room and we decided to display the following simple diagram (Figure 3.1) on the wall for when the group came back.

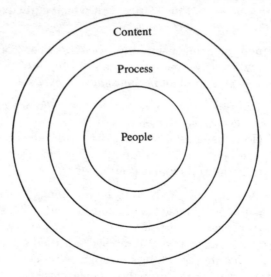

Figure 3.1   *Facilitation levels*

The diagram relates to the three levels of need discussed on p. 11, with people at the centre, followed by the process, and finally the content. We wanted to see how the diagram would be interpreted by the group in the light of the exercise they were doing.

The group returned on time, though Bob was a few minutes later than everyone else, and, from their expressions, I imagined that Derek and David were annoyed by this. I asked the group how they felt after the time alone, and we went round and each person commented. When it was Michael's turn he said he wanted to know what the diagram on the wall was about. Everyone then looked at the diagram, and then at me.

I asked them if they would like to do an experiment. There were one or two comments, but they agreed. I then suggested we divide into four groups of three and I asked for four volunteers to lead the groups. Margaret, David, Michael and Sid volunteered, so then I asked them to stand in a row and everyone else to choose who they wanted to work with and stand behind them. After a few minutes the groups were formed, including me and Joe.

I then suggested that each group prepare a short presentation on the meaning of the diagram, and decide how we should continue to identify our own personal needs. We decided to spend an hour doing this. Derek stopped us before we left the main room by saying,

'Just a minute—two groups have an unfair advantage because they have Trevor and Joe in them.'

'Why do you think this is an advantage?', I asked him.

'Well you should know what you're doing, you know the answer', he responded.

'Well, I don't agree', Melanie said. 'Trevor is in my group, and I already feel apprehensive about it, even before we start.'

I suggested that we go on with the exercise in spite of our misgivings and see what happens.

'Yes', said Michael impatiently 'let's get on with it.'

So we did.

I am always keen to participate in the group exercises—not every exercise, but those that involve me as a member of the group rather than as a facilitator. I know many trainers and facilitators who would argue strongly against this approach, saying that you cannot afford to blur the boundaries between participant and facilitator. To this I say 'rubbish'. What these people are saying is that they can't handle integrated facilitation.

They can only work from 'outside' the group. This is very limiting. It is far better if facilitators can work from within and from outside the group. I liken it to a mountain guide who chooses when to lead from the front, when to lead from within the group and when to lead from behind. The perception gained from these different positions gives a breadth of vision of the group that is essential for good facilitation. (In his book *The Facilitator's Handbook*, John Heron refers to these three positions as the **hierarchical mode**—in front; the **cooperative mode**—within; and the **autonomous mode**—behind.)

We returned to the main room, more or less on time. We were waiting for the last group to arrive. Once again Derek was agitated.

'Can't they tell the time?' he said, angrily.

'Well, perhaps you would like to get them', I suggested.

'That's your job, not mine', he said.

'But I'm not the person who is irritated', I told him.

'No, but you are supposed to be the facilitator', he accused.

'Would you like me to go and get them?' I offered. But before he could reply the group arrived.

Derek was still angry, so I asked him if there was anything he wanted to say to me or the group before we continued. He decided to tell the group that he always got angry when people were late, and that he would appreciate it if we all agreed to be punctual. His anger seemed to subside, so we continued.

Each group then made a short presentation (the details are in Appendix 3). The main points that flowed from the presentations are summarized below.

Figure 3.1 suggests that there are two main approaches to assessing our own needs. Firstly, we can work from outside the circle moving inwards by looking at the content we want, then how we want to process that content, and finally what impact it will have on us.

The second main approach is from the inside moving outwards, first looking at ourselves, then at the way we process our environment, then at the content that is currently of interest to us.

These main outcomes then led on to a very lively discussion about which was the best way, and what the differences would be between the two approaches. Of course, when we are out of the group environment we can look at such questions in a theoretical way, and I could add what I think is the most appropriate way. But that is not facilitation. I see my role as a facilitator as giving participants the opportunity to form their own opinions.

However, what is clear about these two approaches is that when we approach from outside the circle we give initial, and often most, importance to the content, whereas when we approach from the inside we give greatest weight to personal needs. And whichever way we approach, the process is what makes the content useful to the person.

After the reports from the groups I asked them how they would like to proceed. Jennifer spoke first and said that she would like to prepare her list of objectives and needs, but she would like some guidance as to the format. The rest of the group echoed this request for guidance, and Joe offered to have a go at producing a format. He then drew the following simple framework (Figure 3.2) on the flip chart.

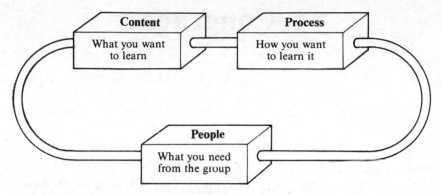

Content — What you want to learn

Process — How you want to learn it

People — What you need from the group

Figure 3.2 Format for objectives and needs

I suggested that rather than complete this on our own it might be useful to work with another person with whom we could prepare our ideas. I left the group to choose partners and I worked with Jennifer.

At this stage in the process I think it is important that individuals are not pushed to being too open in the large group, which can be quite off-putting. I would encourage them to share their personal objectives with the complete group, but they would always have the option to choose to keep their thoughts to themselves if that is what they want to do.

When everyone reassembled I asked them how the exercise had gone. The general response was very good. Everyone commented that they had found the exercise useful and enjoyable, especially doing it with another person. Melanie said that she would like to know what other people wanted from the group. There was some agreement, but Doreen and Gregory were hesitant about it. So I suggested that each person paired off with another person and shared their personal needs, and to keep doing it until they had shared with everyone— which is how we spent the next 40 minutes.

This sharing and matching of needs is an important process which helps individuals to gain some understanding of what others want. This is often the first direct sharing that takes place in the group, and is an important early step in the formation process.

References

1. Hoff, Benjamin (1982) *The Tao of Pooh*, London, Methuen.

4 Congruence

If the individual or group is faced by a problem;

If a catalyst-leader provides a permissive atmosphere;

If responsibility is genuinely placed with the individual or group;

If there is basic respect for the capacity of the individual or group;

Then, responsible and adequate analysis of the problem is made:

- responsible self-direction occurs;
- the creativity, productivity, quality of product exhibited are superior to results of other comparable methods;
- individual and group morale and confidence develop.[1]

When facilitator and group meet in an atmosphere where each is genuine in attitude, response and behaviour, then congruence occurs. This means that participants and facilitators have to be honest and open in their behaviour and actions. When this happens it isn't noticed as congruence, but as a comfortable and productive contact between people, as harmony.

When incongruence appears it is noticed as something unreal, as not making sense, or not 'clicking', or disharmony. Incongruence can be seen quite clearly when someone in the group denies anger, but does so in a way that reflects their anger, or when people say they feel fine when all their facial expressions and body movements indicate the opposite.

In developing a congruent, or real, atmosphere facilitators have to lead through example, there is no other way to do it. People can't be made to be real, or forced to be honest; as Carl Rogers says:

To be genuine, or honest, or congruent, or real means to be this way about one-self, I cannot be real about another because I do not know what is real for him. I can only tell, if I wish to be truly honest, what is going on in me.[2]

To develop congruence I believe in developing a relationship with the group based on what I describe as a 'loving TOUCH'. The word 'TOUCH' is an acronym for trust, openness, understanding, confidentiality and honesty.

Trust   Unless there is trust between the facilitators and participants, and between participants, it will be impossible for any meaningful sharing to take place. Trust is being able to rely on the integrity of the people with whom we come into contact.

Openness When I am open I reveal myself to those around me. I have nothing to hide. My strengths and weaknesses are all on display. By being open I am real. I also need a safe place where my openness will be respected, and where I can trust that I will not be disadvantaged by being open.

Understanding You might recognize understanding as empathy. It means being aware of and respecting the feelings, thoughts and actions of others. It does not mean agreeing with or approving of others; it means respecting where they are and what is happening for them in the here and now.

Confidentiality Part of my ability to trust others is the belief that they will treat what I say in an understanding way and not try to use what they learn about me either for their own advantage or to my disadvantage. This is what I mean by confidentiality. I want to have the confidence to be fully myself without fear of any bad repercussions.

Honesty For me, honesty is to be able to say how I really feel and what I really think, without fear that others will be hurt. However, close congruent contact with other people is rarely free from pain. No matter how loving and caring we might be, if we are to be really honest there will be times when it is hurtful to others. But when I use my honesty to deliberately hurt others then I am not paying them the respect and regard they deserve. To know and understand me you will have to cope with my honesty.

Your pain is the breaking shell that encloses your understanding.[3]

When I work with a group I want to work with a 'loving TOUCH'. I can explain this to the group and I can seek to persuade them that this is a good way for us all to work together. Alternatively, I can model the 'loving TOUCH' approach and gradually introduce some of the ideas it encompasses.

When we reassembled after lunch on the Monday afternoon, Bob was the first to speak.

'I just wanted to comment that I found the exercise we have just done and the sharing very useful and enjoyable. I really feel that I am getting to know everyone much more quickly than is usual for me.'

Then Doreen spoke. 'I would like to agree with Bob, and to say that over lunch I realized that when we looked at the circle I didn't pick up the fact that for this workshop the content is the process, and vice versa.'

There was some discussion about this, and when the group seemed to be ready I asked if they wanted to continue. They said yes, so I asked them where they would like to start.

Derek immediately jumped in and said he had relationship skills high on his list and he would like to start there, and in particular he would like to learn about the Johari Window that someone had put on the agenda.

The group appeared to accept this idea, so I asked Derek how he would like to proceed.

'I would like you to tell us about it', he said with a grin.

I said I had an idea that I would like them to consider. I told them that there was a short paper on the table about the Johari Window (during lunch Joe and I had placed several piles of different papers and books on a table at the side of the room by the door), and I suggested that they each took a copy of the paper and read it. Then, working in pairs, they could draw a Johari Window for themselves and report back on the experience to the group. There was some laughter, including Derek, and they set about the exercise very willingly. (See Appendix 4 for a summary of the Johari paper.)

In the situation of the workshop we are following, where the content is being learned both from the content provided and from experiencing the process, it is important not to let the boundary between process and content become blurred. You may have noticed that when the comment was made about the process and content being the same thing I allowed the discussion to continue and I didn't contradict this idea. I trusted that the group would, in due course, realize the importance of keeping the boundary intact. But I made a note of it anyway for future reference.

Everyone returned and we discussed what they thought of the Johari Window. Some of the old hands had seen it before, but it was new to others in the group. I suggested that we kept our own window handy with our statement of needs, so that as the workshop progressed we could see what changes occurred to the window.

One of the things I like about using a Johari Window exercise is that it supports the ideas of openness and honesty, and hence congruence. But like any analysis or assessment technique it is only a snapshot of how we think things are. The most effective test, especially of how we are making contact with other people, is what is actually happening at this moment. I sometimes find that ideas like the Johari Window are useful for increasing people's awareness about what is happening when they make contact with others.

To become aware of what is happening, I must pay attention with an open mind. I must set aside my personal prejudices or bias. Prejudiced people see only what fits their prejudices.[4]

Congruence does, then, represent the free, open and honest coming together of people. It is about making close and effective contact based on Rogers 'unconditional positive regard' for each other. This means being fully aware; communicating thoughts and feelings, and sharing fully in the experience of the contact. This is depicted in Figure 4.1.

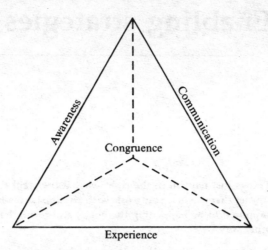

Figure 4.1 *Congruence*

References

1. Rogers, Carl R. (1951) *Client Centred Therapy*, London: Constable.
2. Rogers, Carl R. (1983) *Freedom to Learn*, Columbus, Ohio: C.E. Merrill.
3. Gibran, Kahlil (1991) *The Prophet*, London: Mandarin.
4. Heider, John (1986) *The Tao of Leadership*, Aldershot: Wildwood House.

5 Enabling strategies

Things just happen in the right way, at the right time. At least they do when you let them, when you work with circumstances instead of saying 'This isn't supposed to be happening this way', and trying hard to make it happen some other way.[1]

When people first come together in a group there is a period of time when they are unsure about what it is OK to do and what it is not OK to do. The group can be left to sort this out for themselves by exploring and experimenting with what is possible. This is only one strategy that can be used. There are a number of other strategies that can be used.

By 'strategy' I mean a choice about the way facilitators interact with the group. This can be something that is thought about in advance, or more appropriately achieved by selecting from a library of possibilities as things happen. Choosing the most appropriate strategy is never easy and depends mainly on a sense you have of the group energy.

For me to facilitate successfully, I need to be aware of the extent to which group members are prepared to:

- Take responsibility for their thoughts and actions
- Be in control of achieving their own personal aims
- Make meaningful contact with me and other group members
- Work within the context of the 'loving TOUCH'
- Be prepared to take the lead
- Look after themselves in terms of group interactions and relationships

How the people in the group choose to deal with these six aspects of working in groups indicates the nature of the group energy, which does, of course, fluctuate.

My way of increasing my awareness is to try to foster as many inter-active group sessions as I can in the opening stages of the workshop, with an emphasis on human interaction. From this, I try to become aware of the group energy and respond accordingly. The advantage of this approach is that it doesn't really matter what happens as long as I stay tuned in to, and aware of, what is happening.

Facilitate what is happening rather than what you think ought to be happening.[2]

In Part Three I look at intervention strategies, all of which continue the process of enabling participants to become more fully themselves, and more fully engaged in the group process. Here I want to indicate how I use part of my library of possibilities. I say 'part', because when I seem at a loss for how to respond my unconscious feeds me an appropriate answer, which I add to my library.

The elastic question

Very often when participants ask questions it is more enabling for them if, instead of answering, I return the question to them to answer.

'What do you mean by group energy?', Derek asked.

'What do *you* think I mean?', I responded.

For some participants this can become an irritating, if not irksome, way of dealing with their questions, but if I answer I can only say what I think, and what is important is what the participants think.

Active involvement

By involving participants in what is happening I enable them to interact and make contact with each other. In the above example, when Derek asked a question this is what happened.

'I really have no idea at all, which is why I asked you', Derek replied.

'Would anyone like to try to give Derek a definition?', I asked the group.

By inviting involvement in this way I indicate that what is happening in the interaction between Derek and I is happening for the group as a whole, so I invite them to be part of it.

Surrendering control

Most groups believe, especially at the start, that the facilitator is in control. This is comforting and gives many participants confidence in the group. However, at the first opportunity I surrender control back to the group. To continue the above example:

'I think group energy is whether we are quiet or animated', Doreen offered.

'No, I disagree', Michael said. 'I think it's the atmosphere that you sense in the group'.

'Hey, wait a minute—I don't want guesswork, I want an answer', Derek interposed.

'OK', I responded, 'how can we go about producing an answer that we can all accept?'

After a moment, Doreen suggested that we could form groups and agree a definition. So I asked her to take over the exercise, form the groups and report back in 20 minutes.

Non-rescuing

When someone in the group is struggling it is very easy for the facilitator to rescue them. Indeed, there is nearly always a very strong temptation to do just that. This is not enabling either for the individual or the group. It calls for considerable patience to wait for someone to sort themselves out, or for someone else in the group to come to their aid. In the example we are following, this is what happened.

'Oh! I couldn't do that!' Doreen said, looking horrified.

'No, I agree with her', Bob said.

'So do I', Jennifer added.

'Who would you like to help you?', I asked Doreen.

Volunteering

I have a strong aversion to forcing people to participate. In fact I don't think it is possible to force active involvement. It is possible to persuade people, but I think it is much better to ask people to volunteer, or always to offer the option of saying no. Our example continues.

'Well, I think I'd like to do it with Margaret', Doreen said.

'And how do you feel about that?', I asked Margaret.

'Yes, I'm willing to help Doreen', she answered.

'Good: then let's do it', I said.

Non-predictability

When using enabling strategies as described here there is a danger that they cease to become effective because participants can predict what will happen when they do something. It is important, therefore, to ensure that you switch and change responses continually, always bearing in mind what is happening in the group.

Later in the workshop we are following, Michael asked me why he was always unsure about what my response would be. My answer was simple. 'I don't know myself until it happens.'

Creative frustration

Frustration can have the very useful effect of mobilizing someone to action that enables them to take a step forward in their own growth. When it operates in this way it can be described as creative. This is delightfully explained by Erving and Miriam Polster writing about the work of Fritz Perls, the famous gestalt therapist.

Perls described much of his own work as founded in creative frustration. His intention was to frustrate the patient in his move toward any goal which *depended* on Perls' cooperation. Impelled by the mobilization evolving from this frustration, the individual would crack through his own paralysis and become sufficiently aroused to obtain satisfaction through his own efforts.[3]

Personal responsibility

When people join a group they appear to give a certain degree of responsibility that they would never surrender in other circumstances. I am always amused that people who badly want to use the toilet will wait and wait until finally someone asks for a 'comfort' break. Similarly people will ask when the 'tea break' is, and will sit meekly and wait no matter how strong the need.

This is not enabling. People can be encouraged from the beginning to leave the group to satisfy whatever need is uppermost in their minds. While this need is so strong they won't be able to concentrate on what is happening.

Leadership

We are all leaders. When the moment arrives that needs the particular mix of skills, attitudes and beliefs that we possess we will take the lead. Good facilitation means watching for opportunities for people to take the lead and giving them the opportunity. From this can grow very powerful levels of confidence and self-regard. In our example this is what happened.

Doreen and Margaret spent some time talking together and then they came back to the group and suggested that we should first of all work in pairs to produce a one sentence definition of 'group energy'. Then each pair would find another pair to make four who would combine their definitions into a single sentence. Then the three groups would write their sentences on a flip chart and the group would reassemble to create a single definition from the three.

We followed this suggestion, and after an enjoyable and noisy half hour we came back together. Doreen then stood by the flip chart and managed a very interactive discussion until we arrived at a single sentence for defining 'group energy', which was:

Group energy is a moment-to-moment fluctuating balance of mental, emotional and physical intensity and vitality that can be felt like a positive or negative electrical charge in the air as if the group is switched on or off.

After we agreed this definition I looked around the group and I imagined that every face reflected pleasure and satisfaction. Joe asked how they felt the exercise had gone, and everyone said it was excellent and thanked Doreen and Margaret. Doreen was positively beaming.

Enabling people to look after themselves and to get what they want in the way that they want is perhaps the facilitator's most important, if not only, responsibility. It is also difficult to accomplish. It is much easier, and much less effective, to tell them what to do. Leading people by the hand through the minefield of experience is one way to facilitate. A more effective, and sometimes more painful way, is to provide people with experiences for them to stumble through and survive.

Making people do what you think they ought to do does not lead towards clarity and consciousness. While they may do what you tell them to do at any time, they will cringe inwardly, grow confused, and plot revenge.[3]

References

1. Hoff, Benjamin (1982) *The Tao of Pooh*, London: Methuen.
2. Heider, John (1986) *The Tao of Leadership*, Aldershot: Wildwood House.
3. Polster, E. and Polster, M. (1974) *Gestalt Therapy Integrated*, London: Vintage.

PART TWO

Facilitation skills

'Having trouble, Piglet?'

'The lid on this jar is stuck', gasped Piglet.

'Yes, it . . . is, isn't it. Here, Pooh, you open it'. (Pop)

'Thanks, Pooh', said Piglet.

'Nothing, really', said Pooh.

'How did you get that lid off?', asked Tigger.

'It's easy', said Pooh. 'You just twist on it like this, until you can't twist any harder. Then you take a deep breath and, as you let it out, twist. That's all.'[1]

There is a moment just before success when, if we stop or hesitate, or try too hard, we will fail. Facilitation is like this, and perhaps the art of facilitation lies in recognizing these moments. It is very hard to describe when these moments occur, or how to spot them, and so facilitation is itself hard to define, but we can learn a lot from trying.

I once described facilitation as 'non-active participative leadership'; on another occasion I described it as 'gentle persuasion'; and on yet another occasion as 'interactive intervention and guidance'. These various attempts of mine to define facilitation are all inadequate, and only reflect my own perception and experience. So in attempting to define facilitation, and to describe the skills needed, I am aware that I am entering a minefield of ideas and opinions, all of which are perfectly valid.

In this part, as we travel together through this minefield, we will look at a definition of facilitation, and how it differs from manipulation and conditioning. The skills I offer are those I have found most useful. They may be of use to you if you combine them with your own unique way of doing things.

References   1. Hoff, Benjamin (1982) *The Tao of Pooh*, London: Methuen.

6 Facilitation defined

Facilitation is a word which describes an activity. It is something that someone does. It is a process. Yet it also includes non-action, silence and even the facilitator's absence.

Carl Rogers, in his book *The Freedom to Learn*, talked about people having freedom to '. . . learn what we wish as we wish'. For this to happen the right atmosphere has to be developed so that the facilitator can concentrate on providing the resources and opportunities for learning to take place, rather than 'manage and control' learning. Here is how Rogers described one of his courses and his role as facilitator:

This course has the title 'Personality Theory'. But what we do with this course is up to us. We can build it around the goals we want to achieve, within that very general area. We can conduct it the way we want to. We can decide mutually how we wish to handle these bugaboos of exams and grades. I have many resources that I have on tap to be available, and I can help you find others. I believe I am one of the resources, and I am available to you to the extent that you wish. But this is our class. So what do we want to make of it?[1]

The word facilitate comes from the Latin *facilis* which means 'to make easy'. The dictionary definitions vary. Here are three:

'To free from difficulties and obstacles, to make easy.'
'To lessen the labour of.'
'To render easier, to promote, help forward.'

None of these satisfies me, nor do they hint at the empowerment of individuals to achieve for themselves, and it is this latter aspect which is for me the key to facilitation.

At dinner on Monday evening the group energy was high, and there was an air of fun and excitement. I was sitting next to Derek and Melanie. Derek, in contrast to everyone else, was still dressed formally in suit and tie and wearing his badge. Several comments were made in his direction about relaxing, and being stuffy. Derek turned to me and said, 'Is there any rule about dress?'.

'No', I replied, 'you can wear what you want. Why do you ask?'.

'Well, on the courses I run we usually wear a jacket and tie for dinner', he answered.

I told him that I never set any rules about dress, behaviour, drinking etc. I explained that I believed that individuals are quite able to make their own decisions about such things. Then he asked me if I had noticed his badge.

'Yes, I have. Why?'.

'Well, I believe it is important that we are able to identify each other easily', he responded, 'and you don't seem to agree'.

'Oh, but I do agree with you. However, I believe that it is important that we make good contact with each other, and badges act as barriers to good contact. Without a badge', I continued, 'everyone has to ask, and learn who the other people are. If I can avoid this by reading your badge I am avoiding making contact with you. So in order to facilitate good contact I don't use badges.

Melanie, who had been listening, said, 'So sometimes to facilitate something to happen you do nothing'.

'Yes', I replied, 'and this is perhaps the most important thing to learn about facilitation.'

It puzzles people at first, to see how little the able leader actually does, and yet how much gets done.[2]

There are many similarities between what people often describe as leadership and facilitation. These similarities are to do with the way that the process is carried through. However, for some people leadership means being able to direct and move a group in a direction which the leader decides is appropriate. This is only one form of leadership. It is sometimes useful but is often not very effective.

Facilitation is about empowering people to take control and responsibility for their own efforts and achievements. If we grow and develop as people we do so because we make a choice to do. We cannot be 'developed' by others. Good leaders know this. Around 500 BC, Lao Tzu is believed to have written the *Tao Teh Ching*. It describes a philosophy for life, The Way. Here is Chapter 17, about leadership:

A leader is best
When people barely know that he exists,
Not so good when people obey and acclaim him,
Worst when they despise him.
'Fail to honour people,
They fail to honour you;'
But of a good leader, who talks little,
When his work is done, his aim fulfilled,
They will all say, 'We did this ourselves.'[3]

Facilitation echoes this message from Lao Tzu by trying to determine 'the way' that the groups want to go, and by trying to encourage and support them in this process. This does mean sometimes leading from the front, but it is how we do this rather than what we are doing which is important. Sometimes we have to lead from within the group, by example and participation rather than persuasion. And there are times when it is important to lead from the back, to follow, and by following willingly and with skill to enable the group to lead.

In his book *The Tao of Leadership*, John Heider, building on the writing of Lao Tzu, says:

What we call leadership consists mainly of knowing how to follow. The wise leader stays in the background and facilitates other people's process.

Following is not something which comes naturally. We have to learn to follow. Those of us who learn well will acquire the style, attitude and ability to lead. The skills of followership that we need to learn are described below.

Listening in an open and quiet way. This enables me to hear what is happening and to be aware of the feelings and emotions that lie behind what others are saying. It also gives me a basis for the choices that I can make about what is happening, how it is happening, and what I might want to do.

Questioning in an enquiring and learning way. When I do this, and when I listen quietly and attentively to the replies, I am able to learn and to understand what is happening. This then gives me the knowledge to make choices about what I do.

Communicating my thoughts, feelings and ideas clearly about what is happening. I am unable to do this unless I listen and understand what is happening. When I do this I can contribute and share whatever I believe might be of help. It also gives me a sense of freedom to act as I think appropriate.

Acting in my chosen way and in the best interests of those I am with, so as to achieve shared objectives. When I act I choose, and take responsibility for what I do. This choice is based on my clear understanding of what is happening and on the clarity with which I express my thoughts, feelings and emotions about what is happening.

Reviewing what is happening. This is particularly relevant after I have acted, so that I can assess what changes my action has had on what is happening. This reviewing process is concerned with listening, questioning and communicating with others about *what is happening NOW*. By constantly checking what is happening in the *here and now* I can stay grounded in the present rather than keep replaying the past, or fantasizing about the future.

Adapting to the changing conditions in which I am living and working. When I am aware of how things are changing I can choose to adapt my actions accordingly. This allows me the freedom to change my mind and to adjust what I do to suit the particular needs of the moment rather than stick to previously relevant, but no longer appropriate, ideas.

When I am aware of how things are changing I can choose to adapt my encouraged to follow, and so we all share in the leadership. If we accept that everyone has their own process which they have developed as a means of being and surviving, then we need to acknowledge that process and to work with it, not against it. This means that the six elements of followership described above come into operation continuously whenever we make contact with others.

By learning how to follow I am learning how to relate and hence how to lead. Nothing could be more important for the facilitator who wants to give people the opportunity to grow and develop their potential. Or as John Heider puts it:

The wise leader is of service: receptive, yielding, following. The group members' vibration dominates and leads, while the leader follows.

It was 9.15 a.m. on Tuesday morning. The group had assembled on time. One or two people seemed a little worse for wear after a late night. Joe and I decided to sit quietly and wait for the group to take the lead. We didn't have to wait long.

'Well I feel like a nice quiet start to the day.' It was Sid speaking. He was looking tired and decidedly fragile.

'How would you like it to be then?', I asked him.

'I don't really know, but something not too demanding.'

'Why don't you do what you've planned for today?', Derek interjected.

'What makes you think I have planned something?', I asked.

'You must've done, you can't run a course without planning every session.'

'I agree', David added. 'You must know what we are going to do next.'

'OK', I responded, 'If I did have a plan, what do you think would be the next thing I had planned we should do?'

Michael sighed, 'Here we go again', he said, 'throwing the ball back to us.'

'Well it is your workshop, and we do have an agenda that you created, so what do you want to do?', I asked the group.

'I would er . . . like to have a er . . . better understanding of what facilitation is, er . . . if that's OK.' It was Gregory speaking.

'Yes, that would be very useful,' Margaret added.

'Well that seems like a reasonable suggestion. Does everyone agree?', I asked. No one appeared to dissent.

'Now I suppose you will ask us how we want to do it,' Derek stated.

'Yes, that's pretty much what I was thinking', I replied. 'Has anyone any ideas?'

At this point in the workshop it might appear preferable for me as facilitator to suggest ways in which we could deal with the understanding of facilitation. But you will notice that no one has asked me for my ideas yet. If I make suggestions before I am invited to by the group I am pushing, which is exactly what I don't want to do.

In fact, I have prepared in advance for the workshop, but I have not planned a programme. I have planned to have available lots of ideas and materials that can be used if the group want to make use of them. If

I offer these in advance of the group requesting help and support then I am disempowering the group from finding their own way. It is the struggle that is important, not the resolution, though we do want to reach a satisfactory completion of each topic.

The group debated a number of ideas and then Doreen turned to me and quietly asked me if I had any ideas on how they could do it.

'Yes I do have several options', I said. The group went quiet as I suggested that we could work in pairs, and each pair could select a topic from the agenda and facilitate a session on that topic for the rest of the group.

'But we need to know about facilitation first', Margaret said, 'I don't want to look a fool.'

Several people nodded in agreement with Margaret.

'But what do you think of the idea?', I asked

There was general agreement that it was OK as long as they received some input on facilitation.

'OK, then why don't you select a partner, and choose a topic from the agenda?', I suggested. 'As far as input about facilitation is concerned there is a paper on the table which I have written about facilitation skills. In addition, when you have thought about how you are going to facilitate your session you can, if you want, talk to me and Joe about it.'

At this stage in the facilitation process I am working from within the group, or perhaps I am leading from just in front of the group. However, and this is the key, the group is going where it wants to go and using me as a resource to help it get there. In addition, the group working in pairs, are now going to select what topics they address and how they do it. They are in effect taking control and responsibility for the direction and shape of the next day or so of the workshop.

In the paper I had prepared for the workshop I included the following (my own) definition of facilitation:

Facilitation is the provision of opportunities, resources, encouragement and support for the group to succeed in achieving its objectives, and to do this through enabling the group to take control and responsibility for the way they proceed.

To empower people is to help them to believe in themselves, and from this base to explore their potential. Once this process starts it is difficult to return to a position where control can be exercised by the facilitator. In truth, facilitation is not relinquishing control to the group, because the facilitator never had control in the first place, but rather the recognition and acceptance that the group are in control from the very beginning, even if they have to be reminded that this is the case.

References

1. Rogers, Carl R. (1983) *Freedom to Learn*, Columbus, Ohio: C.E. Merrill.
2. Heider, John (1986) *The Tao of Leadership*, Aldershot: Wildwood House.
3. Lao Tzu (1980) *The Way of Life* (trans. Witter Bynner), New York: Perigee Books.

7 Facilitation versus manipulation

There is a widespread view that facilitators 'get' individuals and groups to do what they, the facilitators, want them to do, that there is a hidden agenda that the facilitator is trying to get the group to follow.

This view is widespread because it is exactly what a lot of inexperienced and badly trained facilitators try to do. They do control and influence groups towards the achievement of their (the facilitators') aims, and because they seem to get the desired results, i.e. their desired results, what they do passes for facilitation.

This process of influencing or controlling others to our own ends is what we generally refer to as manipulation. The dictionary definitions of manipulation give us two quite different views of the term. The first is the use of hands to operate and control some process. The second meaning seems to emphasize the unpleasant aspects that many people associate with the term. Here are a few:

Shrewd or devious effort to manage or influence for one's own purposes.

To control the wills or emotions of another person by exploiting guilt or affection, for example, to one's own ends.

To manage by devious, unfair, contrivance or influence.

In my experience of working with groups people hate to feel that they are being manipulated. When they sense that this is what is happening, even if they are wrong, they become defensive, resistant and closed. This frustrates whatever the facilitator was trying to achieve, and thus negates the whole process of facilitation, destroying as it does so any good contact which might have been established.

Manipulation is quite different from direction. There will be times when the group will need, and ask for, some direction. When this is given openly and stated clearly there is no sense of manipulation.

I have found from experience eight situations (there are probably many more) when groups feel manipulated. In each of these the extent of manipulation can be slight or excessive, but it will always be recognized by the group as manipulative.

Predetermined outcomes: if a group meets and the facilitators have already predetermined the outcomes they desire, then it is virtually impossible for the facilitators to avoid being manipulative. Even when these pre-determined outcomes are shared with the group, there is a constant underlying belief that whatever the facilitators do their aim is to move towards their desired outcomes.

Hidden agendas are possibly worse than having predetermined outcomes, because they are kept below the surface of what is happening. Groups are very quick to spot this form of manipulation. Even when facilitators use the agenda-setting process there is a tendency to hold back the fact that they have a programme in mind that they are following. If this is the case then there is an immediate conflict with (a) the facilitators' desire to go with what is happening, and (b) keeping to the programme.

The group returned from their discussions in pairs and Derek asked if they could share with the other pairs what topics they had chosen. I checked that this was what the group wanted to do and I asked Derek if he was happy to facilitate the process. He agreed. Within about 20 minutes this was completed and I asked if the group was ready to go ahead.

'Yes, I think we are', Derek responded, still in his 'leadership' role. 'But before we do, we would like to clarify one or two things.'

'Certainly', I responded, 'but before we do that, could I just check with the group that you are speaking for everyone?'

'I believe I am', Derek said.

'OK, well, let's check then', I said, turning to the group.

'I don't know what Derek's on about', Melanie said.

'Nor I', added Doreen.

'And he's sure not speaking for me', David said.

Turning to Derek I asked him what it was that he wanted to clarify, and this time could he own it by saying 'I' instead of 'we'.

'All right. Well, I want to clarify if what we are doing fits in with your programme.'

'That's a good point', Michael added.

'OK, how many of you think I have a programme that I haven't told you about?' Only Gregory and Doreen didn't.

'Right. Well, here is my programme. We planned to start on Sunday evening and finish at about 4.00 p.m. on Friday. During that time I hoped that we would cover a list of fifteen topics all of which are on the agenda we created together. I had and have no idea how we are going to do it, except that we as a group will decide as we proceed. We are, in other words, creating a programme as we go.'

'Well, I've never worked this way before', Derek said.

'And how does it feel?'

'It feels uncomfortable. I like to know what I am going to do next', Derek responded somewhat defensively.

'And how does the group feel?' I asked.

This question was followed by a discussion about the approach and people commented on whether they liked it or not and how they felt. At the end of this we agreed to continue and to spend the next two hours reading the facilitation paper and preparing the topic that had been selected.

Control of the group process, i.e. what is done when and by whom, is manipulation if it is done by the facilitators without attention to what the group want to do. It can be difficult to avoid taking control at the beginning of a group when people are unsure and nervous about their roles and contact with others. But it is precisely at this time that good facilitators give the group freedom and refuse to take control, even if it means that the group wander aimlessly for a while. As soon as the facilitators take control to give some direction, or to make people feel comfortable, they disempower participants, who will continue to rely on their facilitators. Very soon the control becomes manipulative and almost impossible to pass back to the group.

Suggestions are often used by facilitators to fill voids and to 'move things forward'. This can be done if the group want it and understand that they are asking for suggestions, but when proffered by facilitators to deal with situations of confusion and panic, suggestions become manipulative.

Learn to trust what is happening. If there is silence, let it grow; something will emerge. If there is a storm, let it rage; it will resolve into calm.[1]

Persuasion can sometimes be pushy and at other times it can be no stronger than an invitation. Whether it is manipulative or not depends on why the facilitators are choosing to 'persuade' someone to do something. If it is to achieve something that I want to achieve it is manipulative. I try to avoid manipulation by inviting people to take part and accepting their decision. Whatever situation this creates is something the group will have to deal with, unless, that is, I want to manipulate what happens.

Avoidance happens when I choose not to recognize what is happening. This could be conscious or unconscious, but either way I take a decision to avoid contact with an individual or group. I might do this because what is happening is an area that I have difficulty in dealing with, e.g. anger. So to avoid dealing with it I will move the group away from what is happening and create some new focus. This is a form of self-defence, but it is still manipulative.

Power and authority are not easily given up once they have been enjoyed. They both feed our ego and as such generate an addiction. To be addicted to having power and authority is in fact a very diminishing thing. Far from allowing us to grow and develop as people the addiction acts as an obstacle to our progress. When groups form there are often assumptions of power and authority invested in the facilitators. I have found it possible to get groups to do things that in other situations they would not dream of doing. Because I am the facilitator, the group, initially and immediately, respond to my wishes, if I care to express them. This effect can, because it feeds my ego, make me want to hold on to the power and authority which the group have given me. If I do this then I continue to manipulate the group to feed my ego addiction. I find it interesting that when people meet for the first time they almost immediately try to establish the relative power and authority position by asking 'what do you do?'. It seems that we need to quickly establish our position in the pecking order before we can continue to make contact.

Rescuing people when they are in trouble is a great temptation, especially if they are under attack from a number of people in the group. Rescuing is a particularly disempowering thing to do. When people are rescued they are manipulated because the rescuer is doing the rescuing to satisfy his or her own needs and not those of the person rescued.

Perhaps one of the most difficult things for a facilitator to do is to allow someone to struggle. To rescue people from the struggle immediately shuts off an opportunity for them to learn and grow. Supporting them and encouraging them through the struggle is much more rewarding for everyone involved.

The individual pairs had been working at the facilitation exercise for about half an hour when Doreen and Melanie came to talk to Joe and me.

'We have chosen to facilitate a session about listening', Doreen started to explain, 'and we are confused about what we are supposed to do.'

'For example I think that we could do some exercises to get people to listen using a tape player', Melanie said, 'but I don't know if that's the kind of thing you want'.

I asked them if they had read the paper on facilitation skills, and if they had decided on any particular objectives for their session. They said that they had and that they had four prime objectives.

'How do you know that the group will have these objectives?', I asked.

'We don't know', Melanie replied, 'but we think they are pretty obvious.'

'OK, what do you want to hear from me?', I asked.

'Well I want to know if what we are doing is going to be OK', Doreen ventured.

'I'm afraid I have no idea. It will depend on the group and how they respond', I offered.

'But can't you give us some help?', Doreen pleaded.

'Well, I will say this: in facilitation it is more important to think about what the group is going to do than what you are going to do.'

'Is that it?', Doreen said, rather disappointedly.

'Yes', I replied, 'that's all I am prepared to say at the moment. I suggest that you think about what I've said and finish preparing.'

At this point they both left and Joe and I continued reviewing what was happening in the group.

Many facilitators find it hard to distinguish between facilitation and manipulation, and sometimes the exact point at which the one turns into the other is hard to define. However, I would suggest that any action on the part of the facilitator that moves group members towards satisfying what the facilitator thinks should be happening is manipulation. The important issue is recognizing that this is what is happening. Manipulate if you can't see any alternative, but be aware that you are manipulating.

References

1. Heider, John (1986) *The Tao of Leadership*, Aldershot: Wildwood House.

8 Listening

'Lots of people talk to animals,' said Pooh.

'Maybe, but . . .'

'Not very many listen, though,' he said.

'That's the problem,' he added.[1]

Listening is one of the facilitator's most useful tools. Our ability to hear is one of our five primary senses, and as such is vitally important to the way that we interact with the environment around us. Our hearing is always switched on. People who have impaired hearing are locked out of part of the rich environment of sound in which we exist.

Most of the time we mentally select, from the enormous range of sounds, those which we choose to pay attention to. This process of choice is what we mean by the word 'listening'. The dictionary describes the word 'listen' as:

To hear attentively; to give ear to; to pay attention to.

To make an effort to hear something.

To apply oneself to hearing something.

These all imply making some effort to pick out from the babble of sounds those which interest us.

For facilitators listening is combined with all their other senses to constantly try to make sense of what is happening. So though I talk here solely about listening I am doing so in the context of total sensory attention. Listening is the other end of speaking. Is there any point in speaking if there is no one to listen? There is a well-known Zen question:

If a tree falls in a forest, and there is no living creature to hear it, does it make any sound?

So, presumably, when we speak our intention is that someone else should listen to us. This could be one person, a few or many. And the way we listen will depend on who is speaking, why they are speaking, what they are saying and our current interest.

For facilitators there are probably six main situations, described below, in which they will have to listen. In each of these the objective of the listening will differ.

Monologue: one person talks, extensively and continuously, without any apparent interest in whether or not people listen. This is more a process of saying what I want to say. In this situation facilitators have to listen for the underlying message or reason for the monologue.

Dialogue: I see this as the exchange of thoughts, feelings, ideas and opinions between two or more people. The key to listening in this situation is to grasp what the other person is saying so that a relevant response can be made. There is an implied process of taking turns to speak and listen.

Conversation is less formal than dialogue and seems to be an opportunity for people to engage in sharing information. There is no particular need to respond to what someone else has said, nor to talk about the same things, though there is usually some link between what people are saying. For facilitators the aim is to try to define the central theme of the conversation.

'Not conversing,' said Eeyore. 'Not first one and then the other. You said "Hallo" and flashed past I saw your tail in the distance as I was meditating my reply. I had thought of saying "What?"—but, of course, it was then too late.'

'Well I was in a hurry.'

'No give and take,' Eeyore went on. 'No exchange of thought: "Hallo—What"— I mean, it gets you nowhere, particularly if the other person's tail is only just in sight for the second half of the conversation.'[1]

Discussion: I consider a discussion to be a focused conversation about a particular topic. It is an opportunity for people to offer their views. Facilitators need to listen for the consensus, and to pick out the various themes, i.e. the essence of the group's views. In addition, it is important to notice where differences exist between group members.

Debate exists when there are particular views being expressed for and against some particular theme. The debate might be an organized one, or one that arises from a discussion, but facilitators have to spot the difference. In a debate, facilitators need to be impartial and to attempt to see that everyone is able to speak if they wish, and not just the loudest.

Argument usually occurs as the final expression of contrasting views between two or more people. When agreement has not been reached, and if it is important to the parties engaged in the debate that their views hold sway, then we have an argument. In this situation, facilitators have to listen clearly to what each party is saying and try to define some common ground. Facilitators should not take sides, but remain respected listeners who can summarize and reflect back the relevant positions of the parties.

In all six situations, facilitators can choose the level at which they listen. Other members of the group will also be choosing the level at which they listen, and it is helpful for facilitators to be aware of this as well.

When the group reassembled on Monday afternoon we drew lots to see which pair would go first. Much to their surprise it was to be Doreen and Melanie. I asked if there was anything that they wanted from Joe and me, and from the group. The only request they made was that we should concentrate on thinking about giving them positive feedback when they finished.

Doreen started the session with a brief description of what they were going to do. After a few minutes Melanie started shouting and banging a saucepan with a spoon. Naturally it was impossible to her what Doreen was saying. Then they both stopped and asked us what had happened.

'Doreen was talking and then you started making a din so that we couldn't hear her', Derek said to Melanie.

'Yes, well, that's what happened, but for me', said Greg, 'it showed how our listening can be interrupted by distracting noises.'

'And it also demonstrated how hard it can be to listen', added Sid.

'OK', Melanie said, 'we want you to form small groups—say three groups of four. We will join in as well. Try to consider ways in which our listening can be interrupted, and then report back in, say, 15 minutes.'

We subdivided the group and departed to our task.

Now this subject of interruptions is very important, and we shall return to it later when the groups report back. Before then I should like to consider some of the ways that we listen. My first point is that we hear with our ears and we listen with our minds. It is our minds that select the sounds we want to listen to, and which interprets what the words mean to us. Several people can hear the same word or sound and give it a quite different meaning.

To demonstrate a point, then, let's consider the implications to various people of a train whistle penetrating the evening dusk.

To the saboteur crouching in a culvert it might signify the failure of his mission . . . . To the playboy it might presage the imminent arrival of the transgressed husband. To the fireman in the cab of the locomotive it indicates a drop in steam pressure and the need for re-stoking the furnace. To the lonely wife it means the return of her travelling husband. To the man with his foot caught in the switch down the track it preshadows doom . . . . For another (preparing to retire) it signifies a time for prayer . . . . In brief, the nature and significance of information are primarily functions of the attitudes, situations, and relevant responsibilities with respect thereto of the people involved with it . . .[2]

I believe this is the basis of the old saying that 'we hear what we want to hear'. So listening is a very personal thing that individuals do in a way that suits them at each moment. I have found from experience that people chose to listen at different levels of intensity, and that within a group at any one time different people could be listening at different levels.

I have divided listening into eight levels.

Non-listening occurs when people are engaged with something else that is happening in the immediate environment. It might be talking to someone, or more than one person might be speaking, or it might be because of some distraction. This could include listeners being concerned with their own thoughts or preparing to say something. The end result is the same: the message being delivered isn't received.

Passive listening is a frequent occurrence in almost all contact between people. It can be described as hearing the words, but not the message. It occurs mainly in monologue, conversation and discussion, because listeners do not need to respond and can choose to be passive rather than attentive to the speaker.

Judgemental listening happens when we interpret what we hear according to our own prejudices and biases. It is very hard not to do this. As John Heider says:

The leader judges no one and is attentive to both 'good' and 'bad' people. It does not even matter whether a person is telling the truth or lying.[3]

I personally have great difficulty listening to people making racist or sexist comments. I want to respond immediately and 'put them straight'. But as a facilitator my role is to listen attentively and to put my feelings on temporary hold.

Attentive listening is perhaps the level at which facilitators try to operate all the time. It is difficult and very tiring to maintain a state of attentive listening for more than 30 minutes without a break. For most people the time span of attention is well below this, and is probably no more than five or ten minutes. Attentive listening means being fully aware of speakers; what they are saying; how they are saying it, i.e. the tone and pitch of voice; what they are doing, i.e. gestures, movements, posture etc.; and receiving and interpreting the message they are sending. This is very demanding and takes considerable practice and experience to acquire.

Visual listening is linked to attentive listening, but is used when the words are strange, e.g. in a foreign language, or when the message is unspoken. The eyes feed the brain with the messages they pick up from movement, expression, behaviour, gesture etc. For facilitators the eyes can also pick up activity in the group that surrounds the speaker being listened to. This also provides information about other people's reactions to what is being said. Visual listening is deepest with eye contact, and can also let speakers know that they are being 'heard'.

Reflective listening helps speakers and listeners to confirm that what is being said is being 'heard' in the desired way. Listeners listen attentively and then ask speakers to pause while they re-state what they think they have 'heard'. This can then be confirmed or corrected by speakers so that the message is fully understood. Reflecting has to be done with care so that words are not 'put into' the speaker's mouth, but rather that the same words are reiterated in the way they are understood by the listener. This is a skill that is acquired through practice.

Active/creative listening involves attentive listening, and includes suggestions by the listener about what the speaker is trying to say. This level of listening does put words into the speaker's mouth. Listeners guess what the speaker is saying and then they suggest in their own words what they think the speaker means. Sometimes active listeners give speakers space so that they can agree or disagree with the listener's suggestions. Sometimes no space or time is given and the active listener's view is taken to be that of the speaker. Facilitators have to watch for this happening in the group and make sure that speakers have the opportunity to agree or disagree.

Directive listening means interrupting speakers to get them to say what the listener wants to hear them say. Speakers are not given any opportunity to reply, and directive listeners go on to add their own extra emphasis. Directive listeners use a number of ploys, but the favourite is to say, 'I agree with you that . . .' and then they go on to add something that the speaker did not say, or mean. Facilitators need to be aware when this is happening and ensure that speakers have the opportunity to reply, and/or repeat what they did say.

It is not sufficient for facilitators simply to listen attentively and visually. It is also important to clarify what is being said by reflective listening, and to watch to see what other levels of listening are occurring in the group. This combination of listening to speakers and being aware of the listening that others are doing is what I describe as *facilitative listening*. It calls for a very high degree of concentration and awareness of what is happening in the group.

When the small groups returned Doreen and Melanie asked how we wanted to proceed. Sid was the first to speak. He suggested someone should make a list of the ways we saw listening being interrupted.

Melanie agreed and the feedback continued. After some time, Melanie had covered two sheets of flip paper with statements made by the groups. Many of these seemed to overlap, and some statements said the same things in different words. I asked the group if there was some way that we could summarize what we had. Greg suggested that we could sort all the statements into similar groups and then name the groups. This was agreed and took about five minutes to complete. At this point Doreen and Melanie said their session was ended.

For me the interesting aspect of this exercise was the way that the focus was on interrupting listening rather than how to listen. The outcome has five categories of interruptions.

Distractions can be visual and aural, and either within the group environment, or from outside. Such distractions will have a greater effect when listeners are tired and/or uninterested. The answer is to reduce, as far as possible, the likelihood of distractions occurring.

Speaking is not the easiest way to communicate. People often have difficulty in converting their ideas into words. As Kahlil Gibran says,

And in much of your talking, thinking is half murdered.[4]

People are often unable to articulate clearly, and wander around the point. They way words are spoken and the voice, its pitch, pace and range, all affect the listeners' ability to listen. When other people speak listeners have to choose who to listen to, because we can't listen to two people at the same time, even though we can hear hundreds.

Physical needs also interrupt. If we are hungry, thirsty, cold, hot, need to visit the toilet, or are tired we will need to satisfy the need before we can listen well. Facilitators need to be aware of these factors and to provide the opportunity for people to satisfy physical needs before proceeding.

Intellectual needs will interrupt listening in imperceptible ways. Interest is lost slowly until we realize we 'haven't heard a word'. Now, when I miss something I say, 'Sorry I wasn't listening, could you repeat what you just said please?', which is better than transferring the blame to the speaker by saying 'I didn't hear'. We also stop listening when we are trying to work out what to say next. We can't work on words in our minds and listen at the same time. Boredom is an extreme lack of interest and can lead very quickly into daydreaming; into ways of distracting others; and finally into sleep.

Emotional needs can take many forms, most of which are associated with our prejudices and feelings. When we are listening to someone speak it is possible that what we hear can trigger prejudicial and/or emotional responses. The feelings thus generated interrupt our ability to listen well to the speaker. This will probably not be the fault of the speaker, but rather some re-stimulation of old hurts and messages that we still carry with us. Unless we are able to recognize our feelings for what they are we will not 'hear' the speaker's message. Facilitators have to try to develop the ability to step outside their 'stuff' and continue to listen attentively to the message. This takes considerable skill and high levels of personal awareness.

Listening is one of those special skills that, because we can hear, we tend to believe that we can automatically listen. Yet for many people hoping to facilitate, listening will be the most difficult skill to master. As I write this I am remembering one of today's well worn-cliches, often used by those who aren't listening:

'I hear what you are saying, but . . .'

My response to this is to interrupt them and ask, 'Well could you tell me what you think I have been saying?'. When they try to do this it is often clear that they haven't been listening to a word I have said.

References

1. Hoff, Benjamin (1982) *The Tao of Pooh*, London: Methuen.
2. Dwyer, Edward D. (1961) *Some Observations on MIS*, New York: AMA.
3. Heider, John (1986) *The Tao of Leadership*, Aldershot: Wildwood House.
4. Gibran, Kahlil (1991) *The Prophet*, London: Mandarin.

9 The psychology of language

You talk when you cease to be at home with your thoughts.

For thought is a bird of space, that in a cage of words may indeed unfold its wings but cannot fly.[1]

Perhaps the greatest barrier to understanding and the development of good human relations is the way people use, or misuse language. I believe this is true of all languages, but my experience is limited to the use of the English language. Of course, it is not only the words we use, but also the way we use them that create almost insurmountable barriers to personal development.

Language is a human system where sounds, and corresponding written symbols, which we call words, are used in particular patterns to communicate ideas, thoughts and feelings, and to describe events, situations and places. There are billions of possible combinations, so it is no wonder that, even in the hands of masters, the system fails. There are, however, moments of great oratory and writing when the power of language can move people to great acts; recreate the tenderest feelings; and paint pictures of great beauty.

Most of us do, however, struggle to communicate effectively. For those of us who want to facilitate it is important to recognize the way we use language ourselves, and to watch how other people use language so that we can interpret what is happening.

When people speak or write it is fairly safe to assume that they are trying to impart a particular message to those who listen to or read what they say.

People everywhere can be looked at with the same sensitivity to the way they use language. Some are stingy with words, measuring each word out carefully, like dried beans, or penny-nails, or bullets. Others will pour out torrents of words, like water lapping up and then fading away leaving no trace or like a fling of brightly coloured trinkets, covering up tawdriness, or delighting us in their sparkle and generosity. Some are verb people, some are noun people, some leave out personal pronouns, some will be poetically free, others will be as accurate as surveyors.[2]

For speakers the problem is to find exactly the right words that one or more people will hear and interpret in the same way. This assumes that the people being communicated with have the same system of sounds and symbols as the speaker. The more involved and complex the language used, the less chance there is that it will be widely understood.

Certain groups of people develop their own special words that are meaningful within the group, but are unlikely to be understood by people outside the group. Medical doctors, accountants, lawyers and computer specialists have all developed their own particular jargon. Particular social groups also have their own mix of words that they use when they are together. It is no surprise then that people frequently get 'the wrong message'.

Saying what we mean

When we try to say what we mean there are two aspects we have to think about. First is the content of what we say, i.e. the words we choose to use, and second is the way we say them.

'Well,' said Owl, 'the customary procedure in such cases is as follows.'

'What does crustimoney proseedcake mean?' said Pooh. 'For I am bear of very little brain, and long words bother me.'

'It means the thing to do.'

'As long as it means that, I don't mind,' said Pooh humbly.[3]

When we want to make sure that we say what we mean we need to work to a simple formula. First we need to think what we want others to hear. Then we have to think of the best, simplest, words to use to say it. Then we have to think of how we want to say it, and all of this we have to do before we speak. There is a well-known saying, 'Put your brain in gear before opening your mouth'. Unfortunately, there are times when I don't do this and I have to follow my words with, 'I'm sorry I didn't mean that', and then I have to try again.

As a facilitator, I believe that it is very important to take my time when I am speaking, and to try to ensure that people in the group have the time they need to express themselves clearly.

Meaning what we say

Even when we are careful to make sure we say what we mean, the effect might not be what we expect. When this happens we have to reflect whether we really meant what we said.

On Monday afternoon the group got together and we drew lots again. This time David and Jennifer drew the short straw. They said they were ready and that they would like us to work in pairs and to define the word language.

We spent 15 minutes doing this and then we came back together. 'OK, I would like you to tell us what your definition is', David said, looking at Bob and Michael, who had worked together.

'Why us?', Michael responded.

'Well, I didn't mean you in particular, I meant you in general.'

'So why don't you say what you mean?', Bob retorted.

'OK, I will. I wish you wouldn't be so aggressive.'

'Aggressive!', Bob shouted aggressively, 'I'm not aggressive!'

'Well, I think you're being aggressive right now', Jennifer said, rather sharply.

'Just a minute! Do we really need all this?', Greg said, rather bravely.

'Shut up', David snapped.

'No I won't', Greg responded quietly, 'I would like to get on with this exercise, and this is getting us nowhere'.

'Why don't *you* do something about it', Derek said, looking at me.

'I don't want to', I replied.

'Just a minute: it's our session', Jennifer said, 'and I would like to continue by asking Bob and Michael if they would like to share their definition with us?'

'All right', Bob said, rather stiffly.

They then gave their definition, and we all followed until all the definitions had been heard. There was still a sense of some unfinished business in the air, so I asked the group if there was anything that anyone wanted to say to anyone else, and if there was, to follow the simple three step formula.

David was the first to speak. 'I didn't . . .'. I interrupted him and asked him who he was speaking to. He said Greg, so I asked him to say so. He tried again: 'Greg, I didn't mean to be rude when I told you to shut up, but I was annoyed'. Greg said it was OK. This was followed by a series of comments that people made to each other. Every time someone spoke I made sure the message was directed to the person it was meant for, and that people were saying what they meant, and meaning what they said.

The simplest of misunderstandings can lead to considerable problems, and it is hard to stop and let speakers know what you think you heard them say, before responding. For facilitators the key is to wait quietly until you think you have understood fully what is happening, and then to ask the people involved if this is what they wanted. In the above example in the workshop I didn't respond to Derek because I wasn't ready to do so, and I didn't think it necessary at that point.

The language of power

Using language to tell, push, coerce and persuade people to do what I want them to do is using language to control, to have power over others. There are many situations where people in an implied position of power (because of title, job etc.) learn to use the language of power. This is a commanding, demanding form of language that assumes obedience and gives no room for manoeuvre or response. It is too direct to be manipulative. It consists of words like 'go', 'do' and 'get', which might or might not be proceeded by please. The language of power is spoken in an authoritative way, broaching no refusal.

The language of power has no place in the facilitator's repertoire. Facilitators have no need of it because they can lead by following, and because any authority and power they have is given them by the people in the group. They have no need of the language of power, which only serves to bolster the ego and the apparent power of those who are placed in authority over, but not *by*, those they command.

Questions and statements

One of the problems I have in the way I use language is the way that I was conditioned by my parents, teachers and society to behave.

I was told things like: 'people who ask don't get', and 'It's selfish to ask for what you want', and 'little boys should be seen and not heard', and 'If you ask me again I'll belt you'. With such strong messages being repeated over and over again they became embedded in my very being. So now when I want to close the window in the group room because it is cold I say 'Does anybody else feel cold?'. What I really want to say is 'I feel cold, so I am going to close the window'.

Frequently, when we ask questions we are in fact trying to make a statement, but our conditioning has established such a strong negative reaction to being direct that we deflect our statement into a question.

For facilitators this means that we have a wonderful opportunity to ask people to re-state their questions as statements and to see what effect this has. Usually the impact on the individual and the group is extremely empowering.

De-personalizing language

There is a tendency for people, particularly when working in groups, to depersonalize what they say. We do this by using four words: 'it', 'you', 'we' and 'one'.

'It' is used when we don't want to own a comment that we make about something, e.g. 'It's very difficult to understand what you are saying', when the comment is really, 'I don't understand what you are saying'. Here are two more examples:

| 'Isn't it a nice day' | means | 'I think the weather's nice', |
| 'Isn't it cold' | means | 'I think the weather's cold'. |

'You' is used to project what I am thinking or feeling on to someone else, either a group or an individual: 'You know what it's like when you get tired and can't keep your eyes open'. The statement is really 'I am tired and I can't keep my eyes open'. Here are some more examples.

'You shouldn't swear'	means	'I don't like swearing'
'You should keep quiet when someone else is talking'	means	'I don't like being interrupted'
'You can tell when people are lying'	means	'I can tell when people are lying'

'We' is used to include others rather than standing on our own two feet. Speaking about a problem in a group someone might say, 'We are fed up with you being quiet'. The 'we' in this case is supportive: the group may or may not agree with the statement, but the speaker has implied they do. There is also the royal 'we', when people want to deflect the comment as only belonging to them so they include some non-existing/ invisible person or people for support.

'One' is the sort of word that allows us to be wonderfully vague about who we are talking about. It might be ourselves, or you, or anyone: 'One believes in order and discipline'. This statement would normally belong to the speaker, but there is an implication that everyone believes the same way.

All these words, 'it', 'you', 'we' and 'one', can be made more effective and real if they are replaced by the word 'I'. This indicates ownership for the statement and brings clarity to what is said. Facilitators can help this process by asking people in the group to replace any of the de-personalizing pronouns with the word 'I'. This usually only needs to be done a few times at the beginning.

Limiting language

I am learning, slowly but surely, to stop limiting myself by the language I use. I am doing this by replacing the words 'can't' and 'don't' with the word 'won't'. This enables me to be aware that I am choosing not to do something. Of course, there are times when the word 'can't' is appropriate.

The next limiting word is 'need'. This places me in a position of being unable to do something until my need is met. In fact I have very few needs beyond the basics of life; after those, everything else is a want. So I try to remember to change 'need' to 'want' whenever I am speaking.

Here is a typical limiting statement, which is also depersonalized: 'We can't continue with this exercise because we need to be in a quiet room, and we need more information'. The statement is quite different when re-stated as 'I won't continue with this exercise until I have a quiet room and some more information'. The statement is more direct and clearer, and can lead to some enabling action.

Exercising choice

Throughout my life I have constantly been bombarded with 'have tos', 'musts' and 'shoulds', and this continues in everyday communications. What I am doing is limiting my ability to choose how I respond to what is happening. So instead of these 'choice-less' words I prefer to say, 'I choose to', and instead of asking, 'may I close the window?', I am going to choose to say, 'I am going to close the window'. If this direct state-ment of intention generates a response which is contrary to what I intend then this has to be dealt with and the outcome negotiated.

In facilitating groups the clarity and freedom that these basic changes in the use of language bring is extremely empowering for the group and the work they choose to do together.

Clarity

Facilitating groups is difficult enough without the use of unclear, ambig-uous language. We can help to make sure that clarity exists by ensuring that people are clear about what they are saying. There are three further things we can do to assist this process.

The first is to stop people saying that they 'know' what others are thinking or meaning. Here is an example: 'I know that you think I am old fashioned and traditional', can be made much clearer when it is re-stated as, 'I imagine that you think I am old fashioned and traditional'. The speaker certainly cannot 'know' what anyone is thinking, but can imagine.

The second is to replace the word 'but' with an 'and' when the 'but' is used to limit our responses. For example, 'I would like to do this exercise, but I am scared', sounds and means something different when the 'but' is replaced with 'and', e.g. 'I would like to do this exercise, and I am scared'.

The third thing we can do is to concentrate on 'what' is happening and 'how' it is happening, rather than 'why'. When we explain things we remove the experience of what is actually going on and our awareness is reduced. To facilitate effectively and powerfully we want to keep the focus on the moment and what is happening in the 'here and now'.

There are several difficulties with 'why' questions. One problem is that they smack of causality and lead to a search for the prime cause, the supreme insight that will unlock the mysteries of behaviour and effect instant and effective behaviour change. This path leads to quicksand. Second, 'why' is too easily answered by 'because' responses that place responsibility on external or unknown loci of control. These 'because' responses may indicate rationalization, explanation, justification, excuses, and so on. A third problem with 'why' questions is that they often lead into 'figuring things out' in a cognitive, problem-solving fashion that rarely enhances the experiencing and understanding of emotions.[4]

Perhaps the key to effective use of language in facilitation is to use it in a way that enables good contact to take place between everyone in the group. Anything which reduces or avoids this contact will reduce the growth process. We learn mostly from our experiences in life, which depend for their quality on the quality of contact we have with others. So language can both interrupt and enhance contact, and as facilitators we have to ensure that it is the latter.

References

1. Gibran, Kahlil (1991) *The Prophet*, London: Mandarin.
2. Polster, E. and Polster, M. (1974) *Gestalt Therapy Integrated*, London: Vintage.
3. Hoff, Benjamin (1982) *The Tao of Pooh*, London: Methuen.
4. Passons, W.R. (1975) *Gestalt Approaches in Counselling*, New York: Holt, Rinehart & Winston.

10 Using conflict

There is no such thing as a problem without a gift for you in its hand.

You seek problems because you need their gifts.[1]

Most of us are aware of moments of conflict that we face. Sometimes these are concerned with 'inner' conflict, when our emotions, desires, feelings and thoughts conflict with what we want, or think it is OK for us to do. Many people have such 'inner' conflicts around issues such as eating, and drinking alcohol. But we also meet conflict outside ourselves when we come into contact with people, ideas and situations that we find clash with our own ideas, attitudes and wants.

The dictionary defines conflict in both the inner and outer sense:

Inner struggle resulting from the opposition of irreconcilable impulses, desires, or tendencies.

The clash of opposing ideas, interests, or forces: disagreement: opposition.

This separation between 'inner' and 'outer' conflict is a somewhat artificial distinction. Our 'inner' conflicts stem from our past interactions with our environment which have become embedded in our personality. We have taken in what we should and shouldn't do, and we have been given clear messages about how we should or shouldn't behave. This conditioning affects the way we respond inside to what is happening outside.

'Outer' conflict is that which is presented to us by our current, 'here and now' environment. Though it is coming from outside it is opposing what we have come to believe from years of parental, educational and social conditioning. It is therefore inextricably linked to the 'inner' conflicts that we have with ourselves. The major difference between the two is that 'outer' conflicts can be seen by others, while our 'inner' conflicts can remain hidden inside.

. . . the aim is to shift the 'inner conflict', that between impulse and the counter attacking resistance into an open, aware conflict.[2]

Conflict is a frequent visitor to group work and is, I believe, an essential feature of human relations. For many people the first reaction to conflict is one of dismay and disappointment. It triggers the 'fight or flight' instinct that we all possess. Some of us choose to stand our ground and others to take appropriate avoiding action. In fact, we have become very good at techniques of avoidance. But if we do this, not only do we avoid conflict, we also avoid contact. When working in groups people find it more difficult to take avoiding action than they might in daily life. However:

The well run group is not a battlefield of egos. Of course there will be conflict, but these energies become creative focus.[3]

For facilitators, the aim is to try to focus on the creative aspect of both 'inner' and 'outer' conflict, and to do this by a process of encouraging people to explore the conflict in a safe supportive environment, without protecting those involved.

There is a widely held belief that conflict is bad. In their book *Gestalt Therapy*, Perls, Hefferline and Goodman suggest why conflict is seen as bad before going on to describe how conflict can be harnessed as a powerful medium for growth.

(1) All conflicts are bad because they waste energy and cause suffering. (2) All conflicts excite aggression and destruction, which are bad. (3) Some conflicts are bad because one of the contestants is unhealthy or anti-social, and rather than being allowed to conflict, it should be eliminated or sublimated.[2]

If we as facilitators believe that conflict is bad then we will watch for it, and either try to prevent its appearance, or when it does appear attempt to remove it, or reduce it. This would eliminate an opportunity for real and significant personal growth for everyone involved.

Conflict appears in a variety of costumes. It can be soft and gentle, gradually nudging someone towards the cliff edge. It can be harsh and direct and rush at you unexpectedly. It can be sneaky, and creep up on you. It seems that conflict has almost as many faces as we do. But there is always one thing in common, and that is the spark of opposition. When the spark of opposition appears I know we have a conflict brewing. The spark does not always show up as an aggressive resistance. The resistance might be passive, but resistance there will be.

At this point, when the conflict is apparent in the emergence of resistance, facilitators have to be very careful not to be tempted by the invitations of those involved to take sides. Facilitators always have to remain neutral. If we don't then we cannot manage the process and the conflict is likely to disintegrate into a damaging chaos.

On Monday evening when the group broke for dinner there was still a sense of conflict in the air. I asked Joe what he thought and he suggested that we have a session after dinner to resolve it.

We assembled after dinner as usual. I had not mentioned anything about my discussion with Joe to the group. Joe and I sat quietly waiting.

'What are we waiting for?', Derek said, looking at me. I said nothing.

'We come in here, we sit down, and nothing, just silence. It's not what I call leadership', he continued.

'I don't mind, I quite enjoy waiting to see what comes up', Melanie said.

'Yes, I find it interesting, and I am curious', Greg added.

'Well, I think it would be better if we knew what was happening next', Derek responded.

'What would you like to happen next Derek?', Joe asked.

'I don't know, I'm not the leader', Derek replied.

'Well, if you were the leader what would you do?', Joe said. After a moment's hesitation, Derek answered.

'I think I would continue where we left off before dinner.'

'What—you mean the argument we were having?', David said, with a bitter edge to his voice.

'No, I didn't mean that', Derek hurried to say.

'Well I think it's a good idea', Bob responded quietly. 'I've been talking to Sid and we, I mean, I, think there is a lot more to be said, and I want to clear the air.'

'I agree with Bob', Sid added.

At this point I intervened, and said that it seemed we had two options so far. The first was to continue with the presentations, and the second was to deal with any outstanding issues about today's conflict, and I asked the group what they wanted to do.

'Well, I would prefer to avoid the conflict', Melanie said, 'I hate people arguing.'

'What was it about this particular argument that you didn't like?' I asked Melanie.

'It was the way that Bob seemed so aggressive. It frightened me', she replied. 'He seemed so quiet and then bang, he exploded.'

'How does that make you feel, Bob?', I asked.

'Well, I didn't mean to frighten anyone . . .'

'OK', I interrupted, 'but how did it make you feel when Melanie said that?'

'I was annoyed she thought I was aggressive, and upset that I frightened her', he answered.

'So you now have a conflict between being annoyed and upset', I responded. 'Which would you prefer to be?'

'I would prefer to be annoyed—I don't like feeling upset.'

'Does that mean you like being annoyed?', I asked. He thought for a moment and then said, 'It seems to me I spend a lot of time being annoyed and angry, and it doesn't take much to set me off'.

'So what would you like to do right now?', I asked him.

'I think I would like to explore the conflict some more to see what happened earlier on', he said.

I asked the group if they wanted to do what Bob suggested, and they agreed to continue.

'OK', I said, 'then one way to start would be for each of us to say something about what happened earlier, what's happening now for us, and how we feel.'

'I'd like to start,' said Bob.

The next hour was spent discussing and exploring the earlier conflict and how this had affected people, and how they felt there were issues still to be answered. We brought those issues into the open and discussed them. The emphasis was on what people were feeling, rather than thinking. After an hour of animated discussion I intervened to ask the group if they would like to wind down for the evening.

They said they did, so I asked if they would welcome a suggestion from me. Needless to say, Derek was delighted.

'Then I suggest that we finish by each person in the group taking turns to go round and say one thing they appreciate about each person, including them-selves.'

There was some embarrassed laughter at this suggestion, but the group followed the suggestion and the whole atmosphere changed dramatically, with no sigh of conflict or animosity left.

I believe that good facilitators use conflict to highlight and to work on the issues and problems that are generated. However, conflict has to be carefully used. There are a number of options for harnessing conflict, and these are described below.

Avoidance

There are many ways we can avoid conflict, from running away to ignoring or denying that it exists. Quick apologies and breaking off con-tact also work to avoid exploring the conflict. But of course, as Perls, Hefferline and Goodman say,

Avoiding conflict is avoiding the opportunity for the creation of something new.[2]

Acceptance

Knowing when conflict has arisen, and accepting it without doing any-thing about it also avoids the chance for discovery. 'We shall have to agree to disagree' is one well-known way that conflicts are accepted and not dealt with. Acceptance can also be a form of resignation: 'OK, so there is a conflict, but I don't want to argue'. The effect of such resig-nation is damaging to all involved, no one is satisfied.

The opposite of the excitement of the conflict is the numbness of resignation.[2]

Resolution

Resolving conflict can happen in two main ways. The first is flight, where one combatant leaves the battlefield to the victor, and the second is to fight, where battle takes place and one party is defeated. The con-flict is resolved. One side has triumphed over the other, but is this really a resolution? Perls, Hefferline and Goodman again:

The peace of conquest, however, where the victim is still in existence and must be dominated, is, as peace, a negation: the suffering of the conflict has ceased but the figure of awareness is not alive with new possibilities, for nothing has been solved; victor and victim and their relations continue to fill the news. The

victor is watchful, the victim resentful. In social wars we see that such negative peace is not stable, there are too many unfinished situations.[2]

Completion

Completion occurs when all the people involved have explored how the conflict has arisen; how it has affected people; what they want to happen; what is happening; and how everyone involved can achieve a satisfactory outcome. From this point it is possible to start to work together instead of in opposition to reach a new point of agreement. Of course, this form of completion rarely takes place, and conflicts result in both suffering and destruction.

To reach completion, facilitators have to try to do four things:

- Be completely neutral and not to comment on the content of the conflict.
- To observe the process of the conflict and to be fully aware of what is happening.
- Not to protect either party.
- To avoid offering suggestions about likely outcomes or paths to resolution.

The real creativity and growth comes from the completion of conflicts where those involved have searched for and discovered ways of reaching agreement. This form of personal development is very powerful, but I would like to recommend would-be facilitators not to generate conflict in the hope of creating such growth. To do this is not only manipulative but dangerous, and will be very quickly recognized for what it is, which is interference in the group's process.

Our job is to facilitate process and clarify conflicts. This skill depends less on formal education than on common sense and traditional wisdom.[3]

References

1. Bach, Richard (1978) *Illusions*, London: Pan.
2. Perls, F., Hefferline, R.F. and Goodman, P. (1972) *Gestalt Therapy*, London: Souvenir.
3. Heider, John (1986) *The Tao of Leadership*, Aldershot: Wildwood House.

11 Encouraging confusion

'There's a thing called Twy-stymes,' he said. 'Christopher Robin tried to teach it to me once but it didn't.'

'What didn't?' said Rabbit.

'Didn't what?' said Piglet.

Pooh shook his head.

'I don't know,' he said. 'It just didn't. What are we talking about?'[1]

Confusion happens in the mind when we can't make sense of what we experience. No matter what messages we are picking up from our senses our brain can't make sense of them. We can't work it out. We don't understand. Something is happening that is outside our ability to comprehend.

Figure 11.1 is a simple example of an optical illusion. We think we know what we see, but something about the picture is confusing, so our brain can't work out what we see.

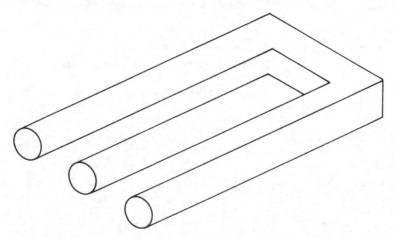

Figure 11.1 *An optical illusion*

In order to resolve the confusion we need to have more information, or to discover what it is that is confusing us and to work with that element of the confusion until clarity arrives.

Few people enjoy being in a confused state. It seems that most of us need to know and understand what is happening, and when we don't we say we are mystified, puzzled, amazed and so on. Magicians and illusionists have made this desire to know into a form of entertainment, and they succeed by not letting us into the secret of what is happening.

I believe that when people are in a state of confusion they have the opportunity to learn in one of the most powerful ways possible. True learning takes place when we move from a place of confusion to clarity. Sometimes, in the endeavour to help people through confusion, facilitators provide too much information and assistance and don't leave people in the confusion for long enough.

People learn and are empowered by being left in the cloud of confusion until they can find their own way out, with help if they request it, but not if they don't (Figure 11.2).

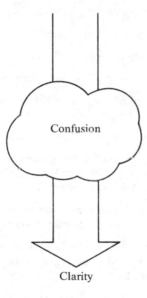

Figure 11.2 *Through confusion to clarity*

It was Tuesday morning and the weather was hot and sunny. The grounds of the training centre looked delightful and very inviting. We were sitting in the training room waiting for Derek.

'I'm sorry I'm late', he said when he arrived. 'I've been for a swim and lost track of time. Sorry.'

We continued to wait quietly.

'Shall we draw lots to see which pair goes next?', Melanie said.

'OK, why not?', said Bob.

Lots were drawn and it turned out to be Michael and Sid. I asked them if they were ready, and they said they were, but that after last night's session they thought they needed to re-think their presentation.

'You see, we picked conflict for our topic', Sid said with a laugh.

'So what do you want to do?' I asked them.

'I really don't know what to do for the best', Michael said.

'Nor me', Sid added.

'Well, I'd like to suggest that we all sit here quietly until you decide what you want to do', I said.

We sat and waited. Michael and Sid spoke quietly to each other and seemed to be becoming more and more uncomfortable with the situation. We sat for about five minutes. Other people in the group were fidgeting and showing signs of frustration. Then Sid spoke.

'We're getting quite confused about what we should do. On the one hand we could do our presentation, but after last night it doesn't make sense. We could choose another topic, but we need time to prepare.'

'So what would you like to do?', I asked.

'We can't make up our minds', Michael said.

'How much more time do you need?', I asked.

'I'm not sure that would help. We're stuck', said Sid.

'OK, then we'll all go and have a cup of tea or coffee, and when you are ready come and get us and we'll continue', I suggested, and I got up to leave.

'Hey, just a minute! We need help here', Sid said appealingly.

'OK, then I suggest you write all your options on a flip chart and select the one you like most. Then come and get us', I said, and I left the room with the others trailing behind, looking somewhat puzzled.

About ten minutes later, Sid came and told us they were ready. We returned to the training room and sat down. Michael stood up and started to speak.

'We, Sid and I, have decided not to do the presentation on conflict, and instead we are going to prepare another presentation for a later session, and for the moment we don't intend to do anything.'

'Well, that's clear enough to me', I said. 'Shall we move on?'

'Why don't Greg and I do our thing?', Bob suggested.

'Just a minute', Doreen said. 'I'm puzzled about what has just happened. I don't understand.'

'What is it that you don't understand?', I asked.

'Well, everything. They got stuck so we left them. Then they seemed to decide what they wanted, and now we are doing something else.'

'Exactly, that's exactly what happened.'

'Yes, but why did we leave them, and how did they sort it out? What happened?'

'What do you think happened, step by step?', I said.

Doreen paused for a moment and then she went through what had happened, point by point.

'First we drew lots, and it was Michael and Sid. Then they realized that their subject was conflict and they didn't want to do it after last night.' She paused again. 'And then I think they got stuck, but I don't know why.'

'Well, ask them', I said.

She did, and they told her that they didn't want to appear to be opting out of doing the presentation, but they didn't want to do 'conflict', and didn't have anything else to offer, so they felt stuck and we were all waiting, so they felt under pressure

'Then what happened?', I asked Doreen.

'Well then you said we would leave them and they asked for help, but you didn't give them any . . .'

'Yes he did', Michael interrupted, 'Trevor gave us the idea of looking at our options one by one and deciding. After that it was easy.'

'Then we left them and they sorted it out, but why did we leave them?', Doreen asked.

'Why do you think we left them?', I responded.

'Because they felt under pressure with us waiting and watching.'

'And then?', I prompted.

'No, it's OK. I've got it now—I understand', she said smiling.

'So let's move on, Bob?', I prompted.

I believe strongly in encouraging people to sort out their own confusion and misunderstandings. I am there as a facilitator to help if they ask, and my help is available, not so much in the form of answers about the content, but as guidance through the process.

When confusion arises, depending on what form it takes I have found four approaches that can help people find clarity. These are as follows.

Explaining what is happening as I see it and getting the people concerned to check whether my way of looking at the situation makes sense to them. This does introduce some of my own views about the content of what is happening, but I always stop short of answering 'why' questions. If I did try to answer why things are the way they are it would only be my own speculation, and would add nothing to the clarity being sought.

Influencing how people see things is possible if I get them to take a different standpoint. In the workshop example above, I could have asked Doreen to say how she thinks she might have acted if she had found herself in the same position as Michael and Sid. I might even ask participants to change seats, or to stand at the back of the room, or sit very close to someone, all to change perspective and influence the way they see the situation.

Encouraging more confusion by asking people to try to make the situation even more confusing than it is. This can be done by introducing more data; taking a completely opposite position; changing the subject; talking at a tangent; or any other way of adding to the confusion. This usually makes the original situation very simple and clear to those originally confused.

Staying with the confusion and just wallowing in, and enjoying it, is another way of encouraging confusion. We have been conditioned in the past that confusion indicates some lack of intellectual ability. This is nonsense. Being able to stay in a state of confusion until clarity arrives is the height of intellectual ability. It is what we call wisdom.

Seeking clarity is done by a step-by-step look at what is happening, and how it is happening. This careful process of sorting out what we see and hear is happening from what we think is happening is perhaps the quickest path to clarity. Certainly, giving people more information when they are already confused with what they have seems pointless, unless the intention is to deliberately increase the confusion.

It is also important to remember that we don't have to know 'why' things have happened to understand them. But we do have to be very clear about what has happened and how.

'Rabbit's clever,' said Pooh thoughtfully.

'Yes,' said Piglet, 'Rabbit's clever.'

'And he has Brain.'

'Yes,' said Piglet, 'Rabbit has Brain.'

There was a long silence.

'I suppose,' said Pooh, 'that that's why he never understands anything.'[1]

Moving through the cloud of confusion to clarity is a struggle, so it is no surprise that we welcome help, and preferably to avoid confusion altogether. But this is not the way to grow and develop as people. Without the struggle to find clarity there is no learning. Facilitators are often faced with people struggling, and there is the constant temptation to reduce the struggle. Patience is essential. Being calm and quiet and standing back are essential. No struggle—no growth.

I do not have within me the path to anyone else's wisdom, but only the path to my own. My role as a facilitator is to try to guide people along their own path, not along mine. We all know the way already. Confusion is like a mist that drifts across our path, temporarily obscuring the way. But if we wait for a while it will drift away and we will see clearly the way forward, at least until the next cloud of mist appears.

References

1. Milne. A.A. (1986) *The Book of Pooh Quotations*, London: Methuen.

PART THREE

Intervention strategies

The leader who knows when to listen, when to act, and when to withdraw can work effectively with nearly anyone.[1]

If there is any aspect of facilitation which sets facilitators apart it is the ability to intervene in the group process in the right way, and at the right time. I don't think I can explain how to get it right, especially the timing. It is an intuitive action. But I can describe the range of ways of intervening, from doing nothing to being highly directive.

This range of intervention strategies has to be practised and experimented with before it is possible for a facilitator to discover how to use them in the best way.

I have a particular style which is unique to me. It might not be a style which other facilitators want to follow, and I would certainly suggest that you allow your own natural style to emerge.

There are six chapters in this part, in which I try to identify and describe the techniques and strategies that I use. These have not always been successful for me, for no matter how well I might intervene, if I do so at an inappropriate time then it will not work.

I present some ideas on how it might be possible to pick up the mood of the group and so choose an appropriate way to intervene. Intervention is the most intuitive aspect of facilitation, and one which it is hard to learn and explain. Perhaps the best way for me to cover the topic is by way of example.

References   1. Heider, John (1986) *The Tao of Leadership*, Aldershot: Wildwood House.

12 Intervention techniques

The facilitation spectrum

Figure 12.1 depicts a range of options from 'doing nothing' to 'directing' and is intended as a guide to possibilities. There is no good, bad, worst or better in these options. However, as we move down the spectrum our input and control of the group activity increases and we face the danger of disempowering the group. The success of any intervention technique is judged by its outcome, and not by how 'clever' the intervention is.

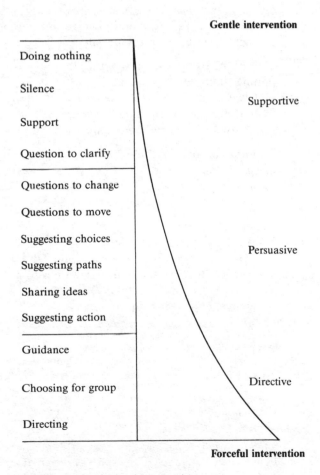

Gentle intervention

Doing nothing

Silence

Support   Supportive

Question to clarify

Questions to change

Questions to move

Suggesting choices

Suggesting paths   Persuasive

Sharing ideas

Suggesting action

Guidance

Choosing for group   Directive

Directing

Forceful intervention

Figure 12.1   *Levels of intervention*

Some of the best interventions that I have made have been largely accidental or unintentional. Sometimes I have unconsciously responded to something with body language, and the result has been quite amazing.

Gentle intervention

Gentle interventions, if they are clear, overcome rigid resistance. If gentleness fails, try yielding, or stepping back altogether, when the leader yields, resistances relax.[1]

The end of this intervention spectrum is the end that I like to work at most of the time. For me it is the most empowering way to work with a group. The aim is primarily to support the work the group is doing. And I divide these supportive interventions into four types.

Doing nothing means literally what it says: sitting quietly and not reacting in any way to what is happening. In Chapter 18 I explore this more fully. The effect is to leave the group to work things out for themselves without any hint from me as to whether I agree or disagree, or have any particular feelings about what is happening.

Silence is saying nothing. I may move, express thoughts and feelings on my face, or use gesture and posture to influence what is happening. See the next chapter for more on silence.

Support means speaking or acting in a way which supports what is happening. It could be as simple as nodding, or as involved as taking part willingly in some exercise suggested by the group. This is the 'going with' the group intervention. It empowers the group and allows me as facilitator to integrate more fully with the group.

Support can be very important in helping individuals to assert themselves in the group process, but when this situation arises it is important to be supporting what is happening, i.e. what the individual is doing rather than the individual themselves.

Questions to clarify provide me with an opportunity to check if what is happening is what people want to be happening. I can phrase my question so as to establish clarity. For example, 'Do you mean that you want to stop doing this?', or 'Is it your intention to tell us what we should do?'. The search for clarity in this way may affect the way the group decide to behave, and so has an influence.

Bob and Greg agree to do their presentation and ask us to leave the room while they prepare. We decide it would be a good time for tea and coffee, so we agree on a 15 minute break. At this stage we have no idea what their chosen topic is.

When we return the seats have been arranged with tables similar to a typical classroom. Bob and Greg have changed into suits and ties and look very formal. Greg starts to speak.

'Good morning, boys and girls.' We all chorus back with 'Good morning, sir', immediately entering into the spirit of the environment they have set up.

'Today we are going to talk about discipline', Greg continues.

'No we're not', Bob interrupts, 'We're going to talk about aerodynamics.'

'Yes that's right', Greg blusters, 'The discipline of aerodynamics.'

There is some laughter and the group start to react with comments and childish gestures and responses. There is a sheet of paper on each table and Bob starts to demonstrate how to make a paper aeroplane. He asks us to follow him and we all make a paper aeroplane. Then he asks for volunteers to test them. We all have a go at launching our efforts and there is a lot of laughter and ribald comments about the results. After about ten minutes of this Bob calls order and we all sit down again.

'Now', Bob starts a little breathless after his exertion, 'We want to examine what we have just been doing.'

'Excuse me', I said, 'but do you mean comment about making and playing with paper aeroplanes, or what you and Greg have been doing for your session?'

'Oh! I mean what we have been doing for our session', he replied, and so that's what we did.

Persuasive interventions

Persuasive interventions are intended to influence the group in respect to what actions they may take next. The level of influence depends on how much power and authority the group have invested in the facilitators. If this is significant then even the gentlest persuasion will shift the group's energy. The more power and authority the group have assumed the more it may need a fairly strong suggestion to have any impact. The range of persuasive interventions goes from fairly gentle to quite strong.

Questions to move the group from where it is can be quite gentle, such as, 'are you ready to go on now?', or they could be quite firm, e.g. 'are you ready to go on yet?'. More will be said on this in Chapter 14.

Questions on where next are more specific than moving on. They seek to establish the next place the group wants to be. For example, by asking 'OK: so where do you want to go now?', the move on is assumed and the emphasis is on where, not whether. Again, this will be discussed further in Chapter 14.

Suggesting choices is halfway along the spectrum and will have a direct impact on what the group decides to do next. By limiting the choices this intervention can become manipulative, so suggestions have to be made with full awareness of the possibilities they open up or close down.

Good leadership consists of motivating people to their highest levels by offering them opportunities not obligations.[1]

Suggesting paths that the group might follow can affect the whole balance of the work the group is doing. I would only do this if the group had clearly lost their way, and agreed that they would welcome some suggestion on the path to take. In using this intervention I would still try to offer a range of possible paths so that the group could choose which one they wanted to follow.

Sharing ideas may seem to be a gentler form of intervention than where I have placed it in the spectrum. However, it is important to remember that if I share my ideas about what is happening the group may take them as an assessment. As soon as I say, 'Well I think', then the group are almost certain to listen and respond. This again depends upon how much power and authority they have taken to themselves, and on how much or little I have intervened in their process.

Run an honest open group. Your job is to facilitate and illuminate what is happening. Interfere as little as possible. Interference, however brilliant, creates a dependency on the leader.[1]

Suggesting action is the most persuasive intervention. I use it when the group is completely at a loss for what to do next, or when the group energy is low. I always try to offer at least three options, which gives the group two choices. If I only offer one possibility then the group has no choice at all.

Directive interventions

Too much force will backfire. Constant interactions and instigations will not make a good group. They will spoil a group. The best group process is delicate. It cannot be pushed around.[1]

Directive interventions are, for me, very much a last resort. When I feel they are necessary I make them firmly. I can be forceful when I have to, but I try to use all other forms of intervention before being directive.

Guiding the group: I guide the group when it asks me to, and/or when it is clear to me that guidance will help the group to move forward effectively and quickly. My first form of guidance is to suggest what I would do if I were in their situation. My second approach is actually to do something, such as write on the flip chart, or rearrange furniture etc.

Another form of guidance is to work with a small group within the group and give them ideas on how they can lead the main group forward. This is like leading from within the group.

Choosing for the group: this is a further step from guiding the group. Here I am leading from the front, actually choosing what we will do and where we will go. I rarely do this, but I will if asked by the group, or if I see that the group is heading for a cliff edge. My intervention would probably be something like this: 'I think it might be useful if we stopped at this point and looked at what is happening. I have a sense that we are heading for problems, and I would like us to reflect for a moment'. This is making a definite choice for the group. What happens next will be the direct result of the choice to stop and reflect. It may be followed by me making a further choice if the group won't come up with the next step.

Directing the group means telling the group what we are going to do next. This form of intervention is the last resort: when all else has failed, it may be necessary to direct the group's efforts. Often when this happens it will impact on members of the group in different ways. Some people may be relieved, others may be angry, and yet others may close off and cease to participate. With all these possibilities it is not a form of intervention to use lightly.

Even if harsh instructions succeed brilliantly, there is no cause for celebration. There has been injury. Someone's process has been violated.[1]

Of course, the facilitation spectrum is a continuum. The points I have chosen to discuss are my way of looking at where I might be on the continuum. I do move around quite a lot in answer to the group's needs, but I work mostly towards the gentle intervention end of the scale.

I am mainly concerned with serving the group than being served by the group. I have no axe to grind; no outcome that I am determined on, and no particular view of where the group goes and how it gets there. My choice of intervention is entirely based on what I think will help the group get to where it wants to be.

No man is great enough or wise enough for any of us to surrender our destiny to. The only way in which any one can lead us is to restore to us the belief in our own guidance.[2]

References

1. Heider, John (1986) *The Tao of Leadership*, Aldershot: Wildwood House.
2. Miller, Henry (1941) *Wisdom of the Heart*.

13 Silence

Endless drama in a group clouds consciousness. Too much noise overwhelms genuine insight.

Allow regular time for silent reflection. Turn inward and digest what has happened. Let the senses rest and grow still.[1]

Silence is a wonderful moment of calm in the maelstrom of the group's process, but many people find silence difficult to handle. To sit quietly in a group presents many of us with a distinct feeling of discomfort. Once the silence becomes established, after a minute or two, it becomes hard to break it. It is like stepping into a lift with several people in it: if I don't speak straight away it becomes more and more difficult for me to break the silence in a natural way.

'I hate silence', Michael said, 'I just can't wait for it to finish, so I have to say something.'

'What happens for you when there is silence in a group?', I asked.

'I'm not sure', Michael replied, 'but I start to feel tense and nervous.'

'Can you remember when you first felt like this?', I asked.

Michael thought for a moment and gave a wry smile.

'What's happening now?', I asked him.

'I'm just remembering what it was like at home when Mum and Dad used to have a row and they wouldn't speak to each other for ages, and there was this awful tension-filled silence, and I suppose when the group is silent this comes back for me.'

'OK', I said, 'this silence is different. We are silent not out of anger, but so that we can reflect about what is happening, and what we want to do next, so enjoy it.'

Fears of silence can come from many different places. My own fear of silence, which no longer bothers me, came from school-days, when I was humiliated for saying something wrong. So I stayed silent, and every time I was silent the teacher picked on me and deliberately embarrassed me, so I became very talkative, and I couldn't enjoy silence.

Silence in facilitation can be used and/or encouraged for at least eight purposes.

Reflection is the first of these, and is perhaps the most powerful use of silence in the process of empowering other people. During the reflection cycle we allow our minds to drift over what has been happening and to extract and digest that part of the experience that means something to us. This is a developmental process. A means of learning from experience, rather than just experiencing. To be closely in touch with my thoughts I need silence.

You talk when you cease to be at peace with your thoughts.[2]

Meditation allows me to rest and lose myself in my mind. I may concentrate on some particular vision, or just let my mind float free of the physical environment in which I might be. It is a cleansing and refreshing process, and should be a part of all group activities. Meditation is not difficult or mysterious; it is just a simple process of relaxation, breathing and calmness which allows us to float with our thoughts just on the conscious side of sleep.

Thinking about some specific problem requires silence. Without silence it becomes awkward to focus on thoughts which appear in answer to questions that we ask ourselves.

Silence is as full of potential wisdom and wit as the unhewn marble of great sculpture.[3]

There is a great deal we don't know about what we do know. Hidden in our unconscious is a vast store of information that we were born with and acquired consciously and unconsciously throughout our lives but have hardly used. To access this store of information we can ask ourselves questions, and if we have the patience to sit quietly and listen our unconscious will often give us the answer. I suggest you try it.

Awareness is knowing what is happening by using all our senses to concentrate on the physical, intellectual, emotional and spiritual dimensions of current events we are experiencing. To do this I need to be silent. Encouraging others to be silent and to be aware is a particularly useful exercise in groups. It hones and sharpens experiences and understanding.

As an *alternative to words*, silence can be very useful. Used in the right way at the right time silence can say much more than a hundred words. As Mark Twain said,

The right word may be effective, but no word was ever as effective as a rightly timed pause.[4]

However, the key is timing. This comes with experience. But one way to practice is never to be in a hurry to speak. When groups are in animated discussion it is those who are silent who learn most, and when they do speak it is usually with wisdom that they have allowed time to emerge.

Encouraging action can be done as effectively with silence as with words. When people in a group are 'talking about' rather than doing something, more words only serve to deflect them further from the action. Silence eventually leads to their words drying up and leaves them little choice but to act. In Shakespeare's words,

The silence, often of pure innocence
Persuades when speaking fails.[5]

Sometimes I find that my silence, accompanied by a facial expression, is sufficient to effect considerable movement by people who are being particularly reluctant to do something. It is as if my words would invite contradiction and lead to further discussion, whereas my silence offers nothing but an opportunity to act.

Avoiding interaction is also achieved through silence. This is the silence of disagreement. It is a 'tight-lipped' silence. Determination and stubbornness can be seen in the posture, expression and gestures of the person wishing to avoid making contact. Fortunately for facilitators, the silent message is usually so clear that it can be a source of progress rather than a barrier. This is where awareness is so important.

Empowering involvement frequently needs a period of silence for people to assimilate what they want to do to move forward. When people decide to become responsible for their action, they also need to feel 'response-able', and this will need a period of quiet to evolve.

Silence is the element in which great things fashion themselves together, that at length they may emerge, full-formed and majestic, into the daylight of life.[2]

The process of facilitation calls for silence to be understood so that it can be allowed to play a full part in the group process. I like to look at this at three levels.

Being silent is my own use of silence as a means of facilitation. It involves me making a choice about when to be silent and when to speak. This choice is intuitive and is, therefore, difficult to attach particular signals to.

Asking for silence is something I do when I sense the moment is right for a period of quiet. Again, this is an intuitive decision. There are three ways I ask for silence. These are:

• 'Would you like a moment of quiet?'
• 'I think it would be a good idea if we had a moment of quiet.'
• 'I would like a moment of quiet.'

Interpreting silence is the other side of the coin, when the group are silent, or particular members of the group are silent. My first approach is to try to do this from my awareness of what is happening in the group. My second approach is to try to observe how people are behaving or moving, their expressions etc., and finally I can ask directly what the silence is about. Favourite questions of mine are:

• 'What is it that is not being said?'
• 'What are you not saying?'

It is this last task of interpreting silence which I find most difficult. If my questions do not get me a clear idea then I need to try to sort it out. One way to do this is to share with the group what I am thinking or feeling at the moment. For example I might say:

- 'I sense some tension in the air that we are not acknowledging. Does anyone else sense it?'
- 'I imagine that there is some unresolved issue around the anger that was expressed a moment ago. Is that close to what anyone else is thinking?'

In this way I can float my ideas about what is happening without suggesting that I 'know' or 'think I know' what is going on. These suggestions are open for people to agree or disagree with.

I am conscious as a facilitator that I can never know what others are thinking, sensing and feeling. Even if I have a good idea, and even if I am later shown to be accurate in my interpretation, I can never know for certain. This is particularly true of silence.

Silence is a powerful means of facilitation that I believe many facilitators overlook, for how can silence be a form of intervention if I do or say nothing? It can and is, and it has the added advantage that it cannot be construed as interference or intrusion, as other clumsy spoken interventions might be. As the famous proverb says:

Speech is silver, but silence is golden.

References

1. Heider, John (1986) *The Tao of Leadership*, Aldershot: Wildwood House.
2. Gibran, Kahlil (1991) *The Prophet*, London: Mandarin.
3. Huxley, Aldous (1928) *Point Counter Point*, London: Grafton.
4. Twain, Mark (1923) *Speeches*.
5. Shakespeare, William *The Winter's Tale*, Act 2, Scene 2.

14 Questions

For that which is boundless in you abides in the mansion in the sky, whose door is the morning mist, and whose windows are the songs and the silences of night.[1]

Questions are the facilitator's keys to opening the doors and windows into what is going on for the group and the individual members of the group. For me, all contact with people is a process of asking and answering questions. In facilitation work with groups, and frequently on a one-to-one basis, I don't always answer questions. I do, however, ask a lot of questions.

Being aware of how questions can be used, and knowing ways in which the subject matter of the questions can be explored are essential features of good facilitation. But why are questions so important? I believe there are three reasons.

Involvement   First is the need for people to feel involved in what is happening, and an excellent way to do this is by asking questions which invite them to participate.

Interaction   People, especially when working in groups, like to be able to interact with other members of the group and the facilitators. But not everyone feels able to interact freely and confidently. Facilitators can help them to overcome this initial hesitation by asking them questions and inviting them to ask questions.

Discovery   One of the principal ways we find out things is by asking questions. If we have never learned to ask questions effectively, and to use questions as a means of discovery, our learning and personal growth will be significantly curtailed.

Anybody can ask a question, but having the skill to ask the right questions at the right time is essential for the facilitator. This is by no means easy. I have discovered, from experience, nine different forms of questions that are asked in the course of effective facilitation. These are described below.

Open and closed questions can both be used for very specific purposes. Perhaps I should first remind you of the difference between 'open' and 'closed'. An open question is one which invites people to explore what they want to say and to provide answers rich in description. For example, 'What was it like for you when you were 15?'. Open questions are questions of discovery.

Closed questions allow only a limited response, which might offer a choice or no choice at all. For example, 'Do you want to participate or not?', or 'Do you have experience of leading groups?'. Closed questions can usually be answered with a yes or no.

Questions, whether open or closed, need to be participant-centred and tuned in to the participant's reality rather than facilitator-centred and deriving from your curiosity or determination to be proved right.[2]

All the following types of question can be open or closed, but the outcomes will be quite different depending on the form used. Some facilitators insist on only using open questions, but I find this a limiting attitude.

Discovery questions enable people to find things out. They are usually open questions which enable people answering to explore and be expansive. It also enables follow-up questions to be asked about the answer just given, and so the exploration can continue. Sometimes the question may contain a lead to the area of interest that the questioner wants to explore.

It was late on Tuesday afternoon and we had just completed the presentations by the pairs, with the exception of the one from Michael and Sid. The group looked tired, but enthusiastic.

'I imagine that at the moment you are tired, but keen to move on. Is this an accurate assessment?', I asked the group.

'Well I'm certainly tired, and hungry, but we have over two hours before dinner, so I would like to do something else', Joe responded.

There seemed to be general agreement and so we agreed a 15 minute break before we continued.

When everybody was back I asked them where they would like to go next. I suggested we looked at the agenda list on the wall, which everyone did. Then Margaret spoke.

'Could I ask you a question Trevor?', she asked.

'Yes', I replied.

'Why do you ask so many questions?', she said with a smile. Several people laughed and Derek sat forward in his chair.

'Yes, I'd like to know that as well', he said.

I looked at Margaret and I smiled before I said, 'Why do you think I ask so many questions?'

She laughed and said, 'I knew that was coming, but I want you to tell me'.

'OK, I will,' I said, 'but before I do are you willing to do an experiment?'

'Yes, I think so', she said a little hesitantly.

'Oh it's nothing difficult or embarrassing', I assured her. 'What I want to suggest is that we ask each other questions to find out what we want to know about each other. I ask a question which you answer, and then you ask me a question, and so on, OK?' She agreed, and for about ten minutes we followed this pattern. When we stopped I asked Margaret what had happened.

'I don't think I have ever learned as much about someone else or revealed so much about myself in such a short time', she said.

'And what was it like for you? How did you feel?', I asked.

'I enjoyed it very much. It was scary sometimes, daring to ask you personal things, and I was nervous about answering some of your questions', she replied.

'And did you notice anything happening about the kind of questions we were asking?', I asked.

'I think we were getting more daring and personal', she responded.

'And what was that like?', I asked.

'It was exciting', she replied.

'OK, so now you know one of the reasons I ask so many questions. Do you want to explore what the other reasons are?', I asked the group.

Although in the above example Margaret's initial question was a discovery question, I did not want simply to give her information, but to facilitate her own exploration and experience of the questioning process.

Clarification of what is happening in the group is a very important type of question. This might be very specific to check with someone what they said, and if the meaning I have inferred is what they intended. Or it could be more general, such as, 'What do you think is happening in the group right now?'. The intention is to have time and space for clarity to emerge rather than rushing on into the next waterfall of words.

Moving the group forward can be achieved more easily, and with more respect, by asking questions than by giving directions. This is one of those places where closed questions can be used to limit the choice, e.g. 'Do you want to go on, or stop for lunch?'. Alternatively, an open question can be used, such as, 'What would you like to do next?'. If the group is not ready to move on and you think they are, giving them the option to say no or to choose to stay in the same place is important. Both the examples I have used here do this.

Where to go next is different from a 'moving question' because the desire to move forward is assumed, or has already been agreed. So in this case we want to know where to go. Once again it can be achieved with open or closed questions. If the group are unsure, I often ask them to sit quietly and ask themselves the question, 'Where would I like to go next?', or 'What would I like to do next?'. When they have had time to reflect I ask them to write down their choice. I get someone to volunteer to collect the sheets of paper, to fold them up and to put them in a container of some kind. Then someone else chooses one of the papers. I then ask whose choice it was, and start by asking them why they chose that topic.

Avoiding contact can be done using questions to deflect people away from me, or to depersonalize what is happening. I do this when I use questions instead of making statements, e.g. 'Would anyone like a comfort break?', when I mean to say, 'I want a comfort break' (see Chapter 9).

Asking questions instead of making statements is another way of keeping on the cool side of contactfullness. It is anti-commitment and deceptive, because one is implying, by the question, uncertainty and tentativeness. But the real message comes across because implications are read into the questions anyhow.[3]

Confronting can be done effectively with questions, which can be directed at the centre of the confrontation, either between members of the group, or members and facilitators. These questions are directed towards gaining a clear understanding of what is happening, and focusing attention on the confrontation rather than trying to sidestep it, or sweep it under the carpet.

Aiming the question is in the hierarchical [directive] mode, but the main intent of the question is co-operative: to prompt, encourage, and elicit; to invite the recipient to participate in uncovering learning.[2]

Empowering questions are used to give the group confidence to do something which it is doubtful it can do. In the above workshop example, when the group agreed to continue exploring the use of questions in facilitation the members asked me to tell them. This is what happened.

'If you really want me to give you a lecture I will', I said, 'but I believe you already know all about asking questions. For example, who knows what kind of question I am asking now?'

'An enquiry', Melanie said.

'To find something out', Greg added.

'So what are the reasons I would ask questions when I am facilitating?', I asked.

Everybody started to talk, so I asked for a volunteer. Michael agreed, and I asked him to facilitate the group so that I could participate. The group then went on with the task very efficiently.

Supportive questions are asked to provide the group, or individual members with the confidence to continue with what they are doing. Supportive questions are usually open (at least the ones I ask are), and they do not replace statements. Here is an example.

The group continued to explore the use of questions in facilitation, and we seemed to have reached a point where we had run out of steam. We had created a series of flip charts with headings for reasons for using questions, and then on each sheet were examples of appropriate questions. Michael was looking pleased.

'So what do you think of what we have done?', I asked the group.

'I think it's a pretty good effort', Margaret said, 'considering where we started about an hour ago.'

'Yes, I think we've done a good job', Greg said.

'And me', chorused Melanie and Sid.

'What do you think?', Derek asked.

'Does it matter what I think?', I asked him.

'It does to me', he answered.

'Then I think it is an excellent effort', I said. 'Does that make you feel any better?'

'No, not really. It confirms what I was thinking', he responded.

'So how do you all feel about the way we did it?', I asked. This was followed by a short discussion about how much they had enjoyed discovering what they already knew and putting it into some semblance of order. Their awareness of their own abilities had increased and they were obviously pleased, and this sense of achievement continued for the rest of the evening.

Questions are very useful and powerful ways of facilitating when used at the right time and in the right way. Of course, questions can also lead us into trouble, or absolutely nowhere, so we have to use them with great care.

'Supposing a tree fell down Pooh, when we were underneath it?'

'Supposing it didn't,' said Pooh after careful thought.[4]

References

1. Gibran, Kahlil (1991) *The Prophet*, London: Mandarin.
2. Heron, John (1989) *The Facilitator's Handbook*, London: Kogan Page.
3. Polster, E. and Polster, M. (1974) *Gestalt Therapy Integrated*, London: Vintage.
4. Milne, A.A. (1986) *The Book of Pooh Quotations*, London: Methuen.

15 Monitoring group energy

When you are a bear of very little brain, and you think of Things, you find sometimes that a Thing which seemed very thingish inside you is quite different when it gets out into the open and has other people looking at it.[1]

Things do indeed look very different in a group setting, and the reason is the impact that the energies of the other people present have on us and our thoughts, feelings and actions.

When a group forms, the individual members bring their own physical, intellectual, emotional and spiritual energy with them to the group. The resulting combination of energies becomes the group energy. We cannot choose whether or not to bring our energy to the group, except by not being there. Once we join the group our energy is part of it. Even if we leave the group, some of our energy stays behind.

This mixture and flow of individual energies and the formation of the group energy changes everyone involved in some way. Exactly how and to what extent this change takes place is hard to define, but whenever we contact other human energies our energies merge and we change.

Because of this intermingling of energies, whenever a group forms, a powerful unique energy field is created. Good facilitators learn how to tap into this unique group energy field. Sometimes the field can almost be seen, at other times felt almost tangibly, and often only sensed in a vague way. But it is there, and it plays a strong part in what is happening at every moment.

There is a view that the energy in the group is both negative and positive, and in the sense that negative means minus or withdrawing, and positive means additional or expansive I agree with this idea. But I strongly disagree with the notion expressed by some people that negative is bad and positive good. Energy is energy. What matters is how well we use it.

In Figure 15.1 I depict energy in the four elements of physical, intellectual, emotional and spiritual which make up the whole person. This holistic approach is a very important part of tapping in to the energy field.

I also show the energy flow in two directions, inward, contracting, low energy, and outward, expansive, high energy. At any time in the group, energy is moving somewhere between the extremes, and may be at a different level for different elements. For example, low spiritual and

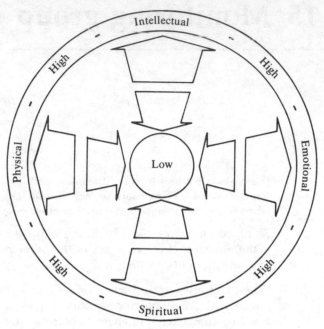

Figure 15.1   *The group energy field*

emotional energy often go with high intellectual energy, and high physical and emotional energy with low intellectual energy.

In order to tap into the current group energy field it is an advantage to consider the energy levels of each of the four elements that make up the whole person, and to monitor the current level between high and low for each element. Of course, it is important to realize that though we can look at these four elements separately for the sake of understanding, they are inextricably linked in ways that we still know very little about.

Physical

The physical element energy level is usually quite visible on the surface, and is expressed almost totally by, as one might expect, the body. When the physical energy is high people are active, i.e. moving about, or restless if prevented from physical action. Gestures are expansive, bodies bend and sway and there is a visual perception of trees swaying in a wind.

People will also be impatient and eager to do things, and there will be laughter and joking in the group. If this physical energy is constrained it will build up eventually to explosive levels. This is one of the reasons why a class of students who have been kept quiet and still in the classroom literally erupt into the playground.

When the physical energy level is low it is displayed quite visibly by people dozing off, slouching in seats or lying down on cushions. The participants can be seen to be withdrawing their physical energy from the group. It might start with one person and then spread through the group. If one person displays low physical energy and the others high energy levels it can be quite annoying for the energized members of the group, because one of them is clearly withdrawing from the group.

Intellectual

The intellectual energy level is displayed by the extent to which members of the group are inquisitive, questioning, or thoughtful. A high level would be constant questioning and searching for information, often towards solving some problem. The low levels are evident when people are thinking quietly, reflecting about what has been happening.

When the intellectual energy level is high there can be a 'heady' atmosphere in the group. People speak quickly, and there is little space and no silence. This can escalate to the point where people are talking across one another and listening is minimal. This level can frequently coincide with high physical energy levels, and at the end of such a session everybody feels very tired.

Low intellectual energy levels often follow a period of high energy when people are just looking for some peace and quiet to let their minds calm down. At this point concentration is non-existent, and it would be quite the wrong time to introduce some problem-solving exercise. People may be so low that they do not even want to reflect, but just relax.

Emotional

High emotional energy levels tend to appear quite quickly when something happens which affects one or more members of the group emotionally. The energy is high when the emotions are expressed in some way. Strong emotions of joy, anger, sadness, love and hate are expressed through physical reactions such as laughter, shouting, screaming, crying, raging and so on. When expressed, emotions are hard to ignore and will affect the whole group in some way.

Emotional expression is an outward sign of what we are feeling inside. Some of us have become very good at hiding our feelings by repressing our emotions.

What tends to happen is that we have feelings about what is happening, but we don't express them. We bottle them up. There are lots of reasons for this which may be to do with past conditioning and current restrictions we put on ourselves. But whether or not we respond to our feelings they are there, and it is often better for the individual and the group if there is space for the feelings to be expressed.

Resist any temptation to instigate issues, or elicit emotions which have not appeared on their own. If you stir things up, you will release forces before their time and under unwarranted pressure.[2]

Low emotional energy often coincides with high intellectual energy. We don't feel in our minds, and often when we sense some feelings arising we talk our way out of feeling, and the need to express or repress them.

We move from our inner selves into our minds, where we hope that reason and rationality can save us from ourselves.

This inner conflict between what we are feeling and what we want to show others usually causes us to withdraw ourselves and our energy from the group. This move towards isolation is often a move away from growth and development, for it is only when we explore ourselves in the light of others that we truly see ourselves.

Spiritual

The spiritual energy level is perhaps the most difficult to assess. It is a combination of the physical, intellectual and emotional. It is the essence of the person, that indistinguishable thing that is our uniqueness. When the spiritual energy is high, everyone in the group, or most of the group, are 'present' in the moment. They are there as their naked exposed selves: pretence disappears and our humanness emerges.

There is a strong sense of belonging, of merging, of full unrestrained contact. There is a 'buzz' in the air. This 'buzz' may be present as playfulness, as compassion, as gentleness. People can be vulnerable, and release themselves from the constant pressure of playing a role, and just *be*.

'Hello, Rabbit,' he said, 'is that you?'

'Let's pretend it isn't,' said Rabbit, 'and see what happens.'[1]

Low spiritual energy is apparent in the almost total defensiveness of the group members. People retreat into their shells and offer very little opportunity for contact or openness. There is little space in the group for anything other than intellectual discussion or exercises.

Group energy flows

The group energy flows constantly from low to high and back again. At the beginning, the energy level is quite low as people meet for the first time. The group is at this stage a number of separate individuals, who often don't know each other. The energy being brought to the group is separate, and people are watchful and wary and holding back. This can be represented as in Figure 15.2: here we see that the individuals are holding their energy apart and not yet merging with the group energy, or overlapping with other participants. The total energy is small/low.

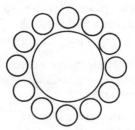

Figure 15.2   *Staying separate*

As the individuals introduce themselves and as the group takes shape the energy levels rise and each member expands and makes contact. The group energy emerges as larger than the group as all the energies combine. This is represented in Figure 15.3: the overlapping individual energies are now merged in the group energy, which encompasses them all. The energy is expanded and large/high.

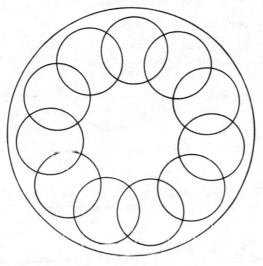

Figure 15.3   Group development and expansion

As the group continues and develops, the group activities pulsate from low to high, like the heartbeat of the group. Each individual's energy expands and contracts as situations change. There is constant flow: a continuous dance as the energy waves vibrate.

As the group grows, a pattern tends to form, with succeeding highs being higher, and succeeding lows being not so low. But this is only a generalized guide: anything can happen.

Wednesday morning started as usual, but I had a sense of the group energy being low. People were sitting, or slouching with heads down. There was very little conversation, and when Joe came in and said good morning there was little response. When everybody had arrived I said, 'I wonder if we can start by everyone checking in with a couple of words about how you are feeling?'

Joe spoke first. 'Well, I'm feeling fragile after last night, and I'm looking forward to a nice quiet day.'

'Yeah, that goes for me too', Bob added.

Derek sighed. 'And I want someone else to decide what we do today.'

The comments from the rest of the group were similar, but Doreen, who seemed more lively than the others, suggested that with the present level of the group energy it might be a good idea if we dealt with 'motivation', which was a topic on the agenda. There were some sardonic grins and a couple of forced laughs to this suggestion.

'Before we actually do anything about motivation, I'd like to explore what's happening a bit further,' I said. 'For example, it seems from everyone's comments that a quiet restful day is what you want.' There were numerous nods and grunts of approval to this comment. 'OK: so how are we going to set that up to suit everybody?', I asked. 'The day is yours to organize as you want.'

'Well, it's a lovely day. Perhaps we could start with a swim, and have coffee by the pool', Margaret suggested with a smile.

'OK, any other ideas?', I asked.

The group were more awake now and Sid suggested a walk through the extensive grounds and maybe even a picnic for lunch. Now everyone was sitting up, and ideas started to come, left, right and centre.

'OK, OK, hang on a minute. We need to make some decisions so we can tell the kitchen and warn the centre manager about what we are doing, so who will volunteer to set up the day's activities?', I asked.

'I'll do that', Margaret offered, 'but I'd like the group to stay together if possible.'

'And I'd like to learn to swim, if anyone will teach me', Greg said, a little shyly.

The next 20 minutes were spent in animated discussion and activity as the day was organized. There was a detailed itinerary on a flip chart, and people had volunteered to make all the arrangements. There was an excited buzz in the air.

Facilitation is about awareness, not about making things happen, but when groups are aware of what is happening they can make changes or stay where they are, depending on what they prefer to do.

Sometimes groups prefer to stay at low energy levels, but often they don't. Low energy is necessary to rest and recuperate from strenuous physical, intellectual and emotional activity, and during such periods of rest spiritual energy can emerge. But when low energy means withdrawing, being disconnected, empty, isolated, closed and heavy the group might prefer to change the level.

It is just not possible to stay at a high energy level all the time. There has to be some respite, and it will come in some form or another. To be expansive, connected, filled-full, outward, open and light all the time is extremely tiring.

The key for facilitators is to remember that it is the group's energy, and it is for the group to decide what to do when they are brought into full awareness of what is happening. It is for the group to decide to change the energy level, not for facilitators to try to force the change because they are uncomfortable with the current level.

The leader does not fight the force of the group's energy, but flows and yields and absorbs and lets go.[2]

References

1. Milne, A.A. (1986) *The Book of Pooh Quotations*, London: Methuen.
2. Heider, John (1986) *The Tao of Leadership*, Aldershot: Wildwood House.

16 Enjoying frustration

Gestalt and Zen . . . both change agents are acutely aware that growth emerges from frustration.[1]

When individuals and groups get frustrated there is a great temptation for facilitators to try to reduce or remove the cause of the frustration. Yet frustration can be the source of considerable learning for everyone involved, and it can be made into an enjoyable experience.

Frustration tends to be the result of impatience, or dissatisfaction with what is happening, together with a feeling of inability to influence events. This is an excellent basis for powerful work in the group, and is generally a signal of pending group cohesion. To stop or remove frustration destroys the opportunity for strong group interaction.

Frustration is defined in the dictionary as:

Feelings of irritation, annoyance, or dissatisfaction caused by an inability to achieve personal fulfilment.

In the group situation things will happen that lead to individual needs and wants not being met. This often arises in the group on an individual basis, but can then quickly spread until the whole group become frustrated. The unmet needs and wants can be very simple, for example to have a break, or very complex, involving past unmet needs.

The needs and wants can be physical, intellectual, emotional and/or spiritual, and can arise suddenly, or be the result of a slow simmering build-up. When frustration emerges it can absorb a considerable amount of energy.

Frustration is usually apparent firstly as some form of physical behaviour, which results in a variety of actions. Perhaps the most common are fidgeting, tapping fingers, tapping or swinging feet, shaking heads and sighing, all of which send messages of discomfort. These are much reduced signals from those we used as very young babies, when we lacked adult inhibitions. Then we could yell, scream, stamp, bite or do anything to draw attention to our needs, and of course when our need was met we stopped.

As soon as the unmet need is satisfied the frustration ends. For some people the discomfort of frustration is so acute that they demand to be 'put out of their misery'. For others the greater the frustration the more intense the feeling of satisfaction. Some people enjoy problem-solving games and puzzles, and could wander round a maze all day. Others are driven mad by even the thought of such frustration.

When an unmet need is recognized and becomes the focus of our attention, for example the need to visit the toilet, it escalates rapidly until it becomes unbearable and the satisfaction of relief has to be achieved. If the possibility of satisfying the need is immediately available to us, then it can be easily met and little frustration arises. However, if there is no obvious immediate way to get satisfaction, i.e. if we have few, or no options, then we tend to let our frustration take over.

Frustration can be seen as a reaction to not having options open to us to satisfy our needs and wants, or at least not believing that we have such options. This leads to us being unable to make choices about whether we stay in an unsatisfied state or not. So in dealing with frustration, it is always useful to be able to meet our needs and wants in as many ways as possible. The more we tie ourselves into one pattern of getting satisfaction, the more frustration we will generate for ourselves.

It was mid-afternoon on Wednesday, and we were all sitting round the pool having tea. The day so far had been very relaxed and everybody seemed to be enjoying themselves. There had been a lot of social conversation and a good deal of talk about the workshop. Derek was talking to Sid and Michael, but most of the group could hear.

'What really frustrates me is the way Trevor won't directly answer questions. I've stopped asking him because I know he'll only ask me what I think, but I'm still frustrated by it. And not having a programme frustrates me to hell.'

Sid and Michael were laughing and the whole conversation was light-hearted. They both agreed that they found this form of facilitation frustrating, but for different reasons. Other members of the group started to say what they found frustrating and our pleasant tea round the pool became a discussion about frustration. So I went for a swim.

When I came to the side after a couple of lengths I could here Derek still talking about frustration. He walked over to the pool and spoke to me.

'You just did it again, didn't you?'

'Do what?', I asked him.

'You frustrated me on purpose, didn't you?'

'How on earth did I do that?', I asked him.

'Well, we were having a discussion about facilitation and frustration, and you just went for a swim.'

'You didn't want me to do that then?', I asked.

'No. I wanted you to comment about what we were saying, to join in the discussion', he said.

'But I didn't want to do that, I wanted a swim. And anyway, how was I supposed to know what you wanted when you didn't tell me?', I said.

He shook his head and walked away, clearly puzzled and still somewhat frustrated.

Dealing with frustration

In the world there are only two tragedies. One is not getting what one wants, and the other is getting it.[2]

The more we are used to having all our needs satisfied, the more difficult it is for us to deal with frustration. Frustration can be a very special moment for us to explore how we go about getting what we need and want in our lives. We always have many options: even when we can't think of them they are there. If we rush through our frustration to grasp at the first chance for satisfaction we miss the possibility of all the other choices that might be open to us.

Letting go is one of the least explored options of frustration, and yet one of the most liberating. 'Letting go' means releasing the need or want from our current focus. If I am frustrated because someone is talking and I want to say something, I can keep trying to interrupt, or I can change my focus from what I want to say to something else. I can let go of my need to speak. When I do this my frustration goes, and I am more satisfied than if I had managed to say what I wanted.

Giving up is perhaps one of the most common ways of dealing with frustration, and also one of the least satisfying and most psychologically damaging. When I give up I repress my frustration; I sit on it; pack it into the knapsack of other conditioned responses that I carry everywhere with me. I don't seek any kind of satisfaction; I simply refuse to continue to be frustrated. I withdraw from what is happening, and I suppress what I am feeling. I don't look for or find any other options; I just pack my frustration away.

Persistence with my frustration means staying with it until I can see some way out. I may search my frustration to identify what it is that I really want. I will look at how I am feeling and explore ways that I could feel differently. I will not seek quick satisfaction, but I will persist with my frustration until some unexpected and unknown solution appears for me. My exploration might include talking to the group about my frustration and discussing how it is affecting me at this moment. This discussion might be about what I want to do about it.

Changing focus: when I am stuck in my frustration it might help to change my focus. If I change my focus what I see is different, even if I am still looking at the same thing. If I focus more closely on something, like through a microscope, it will look different; if I stand back and take a more distant view I also see it differently. This helps me to explore where I am at this moment from different perspectives, which gives me greater choices.

Changing direction is very useful when I am frustrated, because I can move away from my frustration and leave it behind. I no longer have to satisfy the old need because I have replaced it with another that I can satisfy. I can change direction by looking at what is currently frustrating me and asking myself, 'If I can't do this, or have this at this moment, what can I do or have?'. This usually leads me to a successful alternative.

Looking at options: if I have one option I have no choice, and so I am stuck in my frustration. If I have two options I have a single choice of one or other of them, so in order to have two choices I need at least three options, e.g. if I have two options A & B I can choose A or B I have one choice. If my options are A, B. C then I have two choices A or B or C each 'or' representing a choice. When people are stuck in frustration it is a very effective approach to help them to examine the range of options open to them. Most people find it possible to imagine more than three options.

Making choices is only possible if we have sufficient options to choose from, but even when we have we may feel drawn to the satisfaction of the primary need that generated the frustration in the first place. This is where facilitation can help people to look more carefully with more awareness at what they really want.

It was 5.00p.m. on Wednesday afternoon and the group had gathered after a very pleasant day relaxing together, mainly around the pool.

'So how have you enjoyed the day so far?', I asked the group.

The universal response was that it had been great and that everyone felt relaxed and refreshed and ready to go on. In fact, one or two people mentioned that they felt impatient.

'What's bothering me', Derek said, 'is that it's Wednesday evening and we have two more days on the workshop, and I don't know what we've achieved.'

'Does anyone else think like this?', I asked.

'Well I think I'd like to review what we have done', Melanie answered.

'I think that's a great idea', Margaret added.

'I agree', said Greg.

'OK, so how shall we do it?', I asked.

'Oh no, not again', Derek said despairingly. 'Throw the ball back in our court yet again. Are you going to do anything on this workshop?', he asked, looking at me.

'What do you want me to do?', I responded.

'Bloody hell! You really do frustrate me!', he shouted at me.

'So what will get rid of the frustration?', I asked him.

'It's the way that you don't do anything . . .'

'No, I think that's what causes the frustration. You seem to think I should take the lead and tell you what to do next, is that what you want me to do?'

'No, I don't think so. I'm not sure', he answered.

'Well, why don't we look at all the possibilities?', I said.

We then spent about ten minutes looking at all the things I could do, which included producing a programme; telling them what to do; having exercises ready for every session; answering questions with information; and providing notes on every session.

'You know, I think the main problem I'm having', Derek offered, with a sigh, 'is that I have always been against this kind of training. I'm a stand up, tell 'em and sell 'em merchant and I've always pooh-poohed this facilitation approach, and here you are showing us just how well it works, and I don't want to believe it.'

'What is it that stops you believing it?', I asked him.

'I don't think I can do it', he said.

'Do what?', I responded.

'Facilitate like you do', he answered.

'No, I know you can't, but you can facilitate like Derek', I said, 'and just to prove it why don't you facilitate the review session that everybody seems to want, and do it your way, not mine.'

Derek agreed, and the rest of the evening, with a break for dinner was spent reviewing what we had done so far, and what we wanted to do for the next two days. We finished at about 10.00p.m. and at the bar everyone was congratulating Derek on an excellent session.

Satisfaction is not just getting what we want or think we want, but getting something that helps us to move forward, to learn and to grow, to gain awareness of ourselves, and in the process to make better more fruitful contact with others. In the workshop example it was impossible for me to resolve Derek's frustration; only he could do that, and in the event he did it in a very revealing and growthful way.

Our interest in the satisfaction of needs does not imply a philosophy of hedonism. It merely states that if the individual is aware of what goes on inside of him and does something about it, he will feel better about himself than the person who does not possess the awareness or postpones satisfying himself.

The implications of this simple proposition are enormous. If I know what I want, I will not look to other people to tell me what I want, nor will I project my own needs on to others. Existentially, my awareness will make it possible for me to take responsibility for actions I take to get what satisfies me.[3]

Frustration belongs to the person who feels it. It is not caused by anyone else, but is a response to something which is happening which seems to deny the satisfaction of some need we have. To understand the cause and to examine our options for action is an inspiring and creative way to deal with our frustration. I can, of course, allow my frustration to hurt me, and I can blame others for making me feel this hurt, but this leads nowhere.

If I am prepared to listen to my frustration it will give me information about myself, lead to major change, allow me to be creative in my contact with others, and bring me enjoyment in the discovery of new things about myself.

References

1. Seltzer, Leon J. *Gestalt J.*, iii(2), vol. 8(2), p. 31–42.
2. Wilde, Oscar (1892) *Lady Windermere's Fan*, Act 3.
3. Zinker, Joseph (1978) *Creative Process in Gestalt Therapy*, London: Vintage.

17 Supporting progress

'I say, Pooh, why aren't you busy?' I said.

'Because it's a nice day,' said Pooh.

'Yes but . . .'

'Why ruin it?' he said.

'But you could be doing something important,' I said.

'I am,' said Pooh.

'Oh? Doing what?'

'Listening,' he said.

'Listening to what?'

'To the birds, and that squirrel over there.'

'What are they saying?' I asked.

'That it's a nice day,' said Pooh.

'But you know that already,' I said.

'Yes, but it's always good to hear that somebody else thinks so, too,' he replied.[1]

As we progress through a challenging learning/growth experience, we need to find the appropriate levels of support that will enable us to take risks, experiment and explore ourselves more fully.

We have learned during our upbringing how to protect ourselves from danger, rejection, ridicule, disgust and other undesirable responses to our behaviour. We have developed a 'socially acceptable' way of being. Sometimes we call this good manners, or politeness, or conformity, or being inhibited, all of which serve to keep us safe.

But learning is about adventure. It is about lowering the barriers and allowing ourselves the freedom to be different from how we might normally be, and to experience what this is like. Unless we are able to do this our learning is limited and narrow, and has to fit who we have become rather than who we are.

The necessary support for exploring these mini-madnesses may come from several directions. One is the sense that the therapist or someone else is so dependably available in case of emergency that one is willing temporarily to surrender one's customary restrictions—like the Yogi who needs a companion when he goes into the depths of his non-being lest someone cart him off for dead.[2]

Support in the group situation can come from three places: from within the individuals themselves; from group members as individuals, including facilitators; and from the environment.

It is possible for the facilitator to try to set some boundary rules about the way the group will provide a safe, supportive place for people to be themselves. In Chapter 4, when discussing congruence, I talked about the 'loving TOUCH' which is my way of indicating how we can make the group a safe place. In Appendix 5 I offer some more ideas on creating a safe place for growth. Of course, the actual situation that arises will be decided and chosen by the group, which is only influenced by the facilitator.

Inner support

As we have grown and experienced life, so we have developed ways of supporting ourselves. Some of us are very good at self-support. We have been encouraged from a very early age to 'stand on our own feet'. Others of us have been raised in an externally protective way where support is given freely from outside and is always there when needed. The result is that we develop a dependency on external support, which, when it is removed, leaves us feeling unsupported and vulnerable. Between the two extremes of independent and dependent there is a whole spectrum of need for support.

Inner, or self-support is largely based on confidence and self-esteem, and a clear understanding of who we are and our limits and boundaries. It is important for us to know how far we are prepared to go on our own.

Like children, all of us need support from within and from without. A 'normal' adult finds an appropriate balance between self-support and environmental support. We would like to emphasise that self-support does not mean doing everything yourself. It means you have a solid knowledge of who you are and what you need, and furthermore that you are willing to contact your environment directly to get your needs met.[3]

However, even those of us who have developed a high level of self-support will still need the support of the group and the environment if we are to learn and grow. For to grow, we have to enter into areas of activity where we have not dared to go before, and we all need support to take such an adventurous step. To progress in any endeavour means to go further than we have been before.

Group support

When a group is working together to explore and grow, support for each other is an essential ingredient if both individuals and the group are to make progress. Perhaps the most important thing for members of the group to know is that the support is there is they need it. They do not necessarily need to know from which member the support will come, but that it will be there.

On Thursday morning when the group assembled there was a noticeable differ-ence in the level and nature of contact. There was an air of confidence and assuredness. Margaret was the first to speak.

'After the review last night we thought it would be useful . . .'

'Excuse me', I interrupted, 'but who is "we" and what is the "it"?', I asked.

'Oh, "we" is Bob, Melanie, Sid and I, and the "it" is the next session, I suppose.'

'OK, that's clearer, go on', I said.

'Well, we thought that we, the group, could benefit from doing some more practical work in actually facilitating sessions.'

'OK, so maybe you could pose that as a question to the group', I suggested.

'Do you all think it would be a good idea if we did some more practical work?', she asked.

There was general agreement with Margaret's suggestion, but Michael said he wanted to make a further suggestion.

'I would like to suggest that we each think about something, a topic from the remaining agenda, that we think is important and that we want to deal with before we finish on Friday', he said. 'I am happy to do some practical work, but I also want to cover motivation'.

'Could you say that last sentence again, and this time replace the "but" with an "and" ', I suggested.

'I am happy to do some practical work, and I want to cover motivation', he responded.

'Yes, and I'd like us to do some more about fun', Derek said.

'Right, why don't we each pick our topic?', I suggested.

We spent about five minutes doing this and we wrote up a flip chart showing each person's name and the topic. Three people had picked fun, and two moti-vation, and the rest had all picked different topics, which made nine topics to cover in two days, which seemed a tall order.

'OK', I said, 'I have an idea. Why don't we each facilitate a session on the topic we have picked? We will need support from the group to do it well, so I suggest we think about the support we need and how we can get it, and then spend the rest of the morning preparing our sessions.'

There was some hesitant and excited discussion, and we agreed that this was what we would do.

In the workshop example I deliberately suggested that people decide *what* support they needed, and *how* they could get it. I did this because we rarely think about support in this way in our day-to-day lives, and it seemed a good opportunity for people to experience how difficult this process can be. It first means admitting we need support, and second that we are able to mobilize ourselves to get the support we need.

Environmental support

Support from outside the self and the group is the support that we get from the environment, which means from the physical environment and from the people we come into contact with, regularly or spasmodically. Physical support could be a safety harness when working on the exterior of a tall building, or a Help system on a computer. This form of support is usually fairly easy to get, but we still need to be conscious of our need for it to minimize the levels of risk that we expose ourselves to.

The human environmental support is much harder to get, and most of us function in the world with very little human support. This is partly because we have learned not to expect to get it, and partly because we have not learned how to ask for the support we need. It is one of the hardests things to do to ask someone for support, no matter how small the support might be.

Yet we are probably very responsive to other people's needs for support. We have a pride in being able to offer support, but it seems to dent our pride to have to ask for it. There are, for instance, many people in the UK who have 'too much pride' to seek financial support from the state that they are both deserving of and entitled to.

It is a salutary exercise to list the people in our lives that we get support from, and those to whom we give it. The giving list is almost always longer than the receiving list, yet we all need support from our environment if we are to grow and develop as people.

I have discovered that I need support for four primary elements of my survival and growth. These are:

- in being me
- taking risks
- exploring new things
- moving forward

Being me is something I am learning and becoming more and more. I have discovered that most of the real me has been repressed and hidden away by the process of family, educational and social conditioning. I learnt that if I wanted my parents' love then I had to do the things and be the person they wanted me to be. I had to achieve all the things they never had, that they 'sacrificed' for me to be what they had always wanted to be. At school I was expected to fit into a particular mould and to achieve what the teachers had always wanted to achieve, but never quite managed to. And in society I have always been expected to observe the rules and norms of the established order for my class. In all this time I have never been me, only someone else's version of what I should be.

But I was always a rebel, and having survived a heart attack brought on by trying to be what everyone else wanted me to be, I am now finally discovering the real me.

To do this I have needed the support of my family, my friends and my colleagues. Those who have been able to offer me the support are still doing so; the others are no longer there. I believe that what is true for me is true for many others, but to try to be who we are without support is nearly impossible.

Taking risks without support simply increase the risks to the point where sometimes they are not worth taking. This can keep us standing still, afraid to move in case it leads to a worsening in our personal affairs. Unless we take risks we cannot grow, we cannot survive, and we cannot reach for the potential which lies dormant in all of us.

But taking risks without support is foolhardy, and it is not necessary. But some people need more support than others, and it should be possible for everyone to ask for and get the support they need, without there being any reflection on their worth.

I am prepared to take almost any risk when I know that it is safe for me to decide to go no further, to turn back. This is not failure: it is common sense. I know inside how far I can go and what support I need, and when I decide to stop then it is right for me.

Exploring new things is an inherent trait that I was born with. Without it I would have died. I had to explore my world by touching it, tasting it, seeing it, hearing it and smelling it. Now as I explore I need support to enable me to know that it is safe and reasonable for me to explore. But for me the exploration is now more spiritual than physical, and I need a lot of support.

Moving forward: it is easy to stay in the same place. It is comfortable, well-known and safe. To move forward in life means leaving well-known and loved things and people behind. Making changes in the well-known and comfortable means feeling vulnerable, perhaps helpless, without power and knowledge. If there is no support for me in this quest then I will probably not do it, and settle for the familiar.

When I work with groups I am often aware of my need for support. There are times when it is easier for me to return to old ways of teaching instead of working through the difficulty with awareness. I hate being confused, or not knowing what to do next. The first time I told a group I was leading that I didn't know how we could move forward from where we were, was one of my most difficult moments. But from it came a new awareness that it was OK for me not to know. The group supported me and we worked it out between us. I discovered that I no longer had to be the 'all-knowing guru'.

Supporting the group is a primary task of facilitation. It has to be done in a gentle, relaxed way, so that the group know that they have your support at all times, and in whatever situation it is needed. It starts by encouraging them to look inward for their own support, then to look for it from members of the group, and always to know that it is available from you, the facilitator.

The group members need the leader for guidance and facilitation. The leader needs people to work with, people to serve. If both do not recognize the natural need to love and respect one another, each misses the point.[4]

References

1. Hoff, Benjamin (1982) *The Tao of Pooh*, London: Methuen.
2. Polster, E. and Polster, M. (1974) *Gestalt Therapy Integrated*, London: Vintage.
3. Starak, Yaro (1981) *The Counselling Process: A Gestalt Approach*, Queensland: Department of Education.
4. Heider, John (1986) *The Tao of Leadership*, Aldershot: Wildwood House.

PART FOUR

Managing interaction

A leader knows that constant instructions will block the group's process. The leader does not insist that things come out a certain way.

The wise leader speaks rarely and briefly. After all, no other natural outpouring goes on and on. It rains and then it stops. It thunders and then it stops.

The leader teaches more through being than through doing.[1]

I always have problems with talking about managing interaction. The main reason for this is the word 'managing'. I prefer interaction in the group to be a natural response to what is happening; however, there are times when it is beneficial for the facilitator to play a part in the interaction process. Whether or not what I do constitutes management of the process, I find it hard to describe it in any other way.

The five chapters in this part provide my perception of how I 'manage' the interaction in the group. This 'management' process ranges from simply being there to making suggestions for activities, exercises etc. The extent of the management is generally low-key, but is nevertheless a process by which the group hand over the direction it takes to the facilitator.

There is a point at which this management can be overextended and become manipulation. This is not just in terms of how strong it is, but also in terms of whether it is used to get what the group wants, or what the facilitator wants.

References   1. Heider, John (1986) *The Tao of Leadership*, Aldershot: Wildwood House.

18 Being there

Within the group he [the facilitator] is self-disclosing and does not present himself as an expert or source of power. He considers himself a non-authoritarian facilitator who is merely 'there'—with complete freedom to express his feelings, observations, or responses to the group—and a member of a community which runs itself, with its emphasis on the ongoing process and the development of feelings.[1]

The facilitator's presence, or lack of presence, has a direct impact on the group. Yet 'being there' can be exercised in a variety of ways. I have my own preferences for how I am in the group, and these represent choices I make as things happen, but it is perfectly possible for other ways to be equally successful.

From the 'invisible facilitator' to the 'charismatic leader', there are many different ways of 'being there'. A good facilitator will be able to move along the interaction continuum as is most appropriate to enable the group to keep moving towards its objective. When facilitators interact to achieve their own objectives this is manipulation, and must be done with full awareness, and preferably be declared to the group.

The first key to 'being there' is to be *fully myself* in every way possible. I need to be able to respond openly and in a real way, so that the group can see that there is no pretence. Whatever I am feeling about what is happening is shared with the group; they become conscious of my presence, not because of my repeated and overpowering interaction, but because of their awareness of my sustained conscious attention.

The best work often seems idiotically simple to group members who are unaccustomed to this sort of leadership. Yet a great deal happens. Perhaps it looks as if the leader is only sitting there and has no idea what to do. But it is just this lack of needless intervention that permits the group to grow and be fertile.[2]

The group experience my presence as supporting them, without being a crutch for their vulnerability. They recognize that they have my respect and trust to go in whichever direction they choose, and they know that I am there purely to assist them to do just that. They recognize that I am there to sponsor their objectives and that I have no desired result I want them to achieve. Because of this they know that when I am still and quiet they are being guided by their own inner direction finders.

We assembled after lunch and I checked that everyone had had enough time to prepare their sessions. Jennifer said she thought that she would never be ready, however much time she had. There was a general thought that perhaps more time for preparation would be useful.

'OK, I have an idea', I said, and then I stayed silent.

'Well, what is it then?', Derek asked after a couple of minutes.

'Why don't you decide how much time you want, and how we are going to use the rest of the time remaining for the workshop. In that way you will be able to work out how much time you need for what.'

They agreed that this seemed a good idea, and then they sat quietly, waiting, I imagined, for me to say or do something.

'OK, well, while you sort out what you are going to do, I'm going to get a cup of tea', I said, standing and walking to the door. 'I'll be back shortly', I said over my shoulder.

I went and put the kettle on and wandered into the kitchen to talk to the chef about the dinner that evening. As it was the last dinner of the workshop, I was organizing a rather special menu, with wine etc. About half an hour later, I returned to the group. I entered the room and walked silently to a chair and sat down.

The group were in the middle of an animated discussion. Sid was standing by a flip chart with a programme for the rest of Thursday and Friday on it. Michael was arguing that there needed to be at least an hour for closing the workshop. I noticed that the programme was pretty tight, and went on until 5.00 p.m. on Friday evening. I sat quietly and listened to the debate.

'I think we have spent long enough talking about the programme', Jennifer said. 'Why don't we get on with it and see where we are up to later this evening, instead of trying to work every minute out in advance.'

'Well, I think we need to plan carefully, because of the limited time', Michael responded.

'Excuse me', said Greg, 'but perhaps we could aim to start the rest of the programme after the tea break, in ten minutes.'

'OK, then', Sid said, 'Let's just complete this plan and then stop.'

'Right', said Michael, 'So if we allow an hour for closing, and an hour before that for assessment, it means we need to stop the sessions at teatime tomorrow.'

'I'll go with that', Derek said.

'So will I', Doreen added.

'OK, that seems to do it', said Sid, and he sat down.

'So let's have tea', Joe said, and we all went for tea.

In the above example I acted as an 'invisible facilitator' I wasn't even there in a physical sense, but I was there in a spiritual sense, having left the group to complete a task, which I trusted they would do. The group recognized my respect and trust in leaving them to get on with it.

An alternative approach would have been to lead from the front and to have guided the group towards a programme that I felt was both desirable and achievable. I could easily have done this, but I imagine that there would have been a different level of commitment to my guided programme than there was for the group's own programme.

In Chapter 12 I talked about the three levels of intervention (supportive, persuasive and directive), and I gave some thoughts on how these different levels could be done. In Chapter 3 I also talked about the three positions of leadership: in front—ahead of the group; within—alongside the group; and behind—following the group. If we combine the levels and the positions we have a simple matrix, as in Figure 18.1.

	Supportive	Persuasive	Directive
Ahead			
Alongside			
Following			

Figure 18.1 *Intervention matrix*

From moment to moment the group may need or want a reaction from their facilitators in any of the cells of this matrix. To do this, facilitators have to be completely present with the group in the way that the group want, as they want it. This is what 'being there' is really about. The group need to know where I am all the time, and what they can expect from me. Likewise, I have to know where the group are at any time, my position in the group and what I am prepared to give them.

I find it useful when I am facilitating a group to draw a blank matrix on a sheet of A4 paper and to record where we are working on the matrix and how we are flowing from one cell to another.

My role in being there is to be completely aware of what is happening so that I can respond in the most appropriate way. The group have to have the confidence that, through my 'being there', they will be able to explore and develop in whatever way they want.

As a catalyst the Gestalt leader integrates scattered individual themes into spontaneous community creations. This process of transformation is quite complex, and includes proper timing, fluidity of interaction and movement with the ongoing process, mobilization of group energy, and continuous feedback between the group and the leader. The gestalt leader, therefore, needs to be continuously sensitive to the group's emotional and aesthetic range.[1]

References

1. Zinker, Joseph (1978) *Creative Process in Gestalt Therapy*, London: Vintage.
2. Heider, John (1986) *The Tao of Leadership*, Aldershot: Wildwood House.

19 Protecting freedom

The world is your exercise book, the pages on which you do your sums. It is not reality, although you can express reality there if you wish. You are also free to write nonsense, or lies, or to tear the pages.[1]

This chapter is about the freedom people have to be themselves. Unless this freedom exists within the group, there will be no room for personal growth. I believe that a group should always allow and protect the freedom of expression and activity within the group. When this is threatened I feel that it is incumbent upon the facilitator to protect this freedom. This does, of course, have to be done with care and respect for individuals within the group. As groups develop, the process becomes less necessary, but the facilitator always has to be on guard for the reduction or removal of freedom.

So, in the context of group work what is freedom? I believe it comes from an inner perspective of how we choose to react to our environment. If we see freedom only as what our environment apparently allows us to do, then we shall never be free, because there will always be some restriction on what we can or cannot do. Real freedom is knowing that I always have a choice of how I am. This is how Carl Rogers describes freedom.

It is the realization that I can live myself, here and now, by my own choice. It is the quality of courage which enables a person to step into the uncertainty of the unknown as she chooses herself. It is the discovery of meaning from within oneself, meaning that comes from listening sensitively and openly to the complexities of what one is experiencing. It is the burden of being responsible for the self one chooses to be. It is the recognition of a person that she is an emerging process, not a static end product.[2]

The freedom that individuals have within the group, though it is their own choice, can be stifled by the way the group reacts to particular statements and behaviour. If we accept, and many don't, that we all have prejudices and biased attitudes, then freedom in a group means that we can choose to express ourselves as biased and prejudiced. By doing so we can explore the impact our attitudes have on others. We also have the freedom to pretend that we don't have any prejudices, or to lie. In other words, the group allows us to be as we choose to be.

This degree of freedom to say what I want to say and be listened to is not immediately apparent when the group forms: it takes time to feel safe to be free. Nor can such freedom be forced on the group by setting rules. The skill of the facilitator is perhaps the main criterion in how free the group becomes. At the beginning, when people speak they will tend to watch for the facilitator's reactions, and be guided by them rather than by the reactions of fellow group members. This means that facilitators have to be very accepting of whatever appears in the group.

The programme that the group had agreed for the rest of the workshop was placed on the wall close to the agenda prepared at the beginning, which by now had most items crossed off. When the group reassembled we all sat quietly waiting. After a few minutes, Michael spoke.

'I think it would be good idea if we started work on the programme. We haven't got all that long left.'

'Yes, I agree', Derek added. 'Why don't you lead us through the rest of the programme Trevor?'

'It's your programme', I said. 'Why don't you do it?'

'OK, I will', he said. 'The first item on the programme is the subject of motivation, which Michael and Margaret said they would lead. Perhaps we could start with that.'

Michael and Margaret agreed and they asked us to work in pairs and consider what things motivated us to action. We did this for ten minutes, and then we came back into the main group. Derek and Sid spoke first.

'Well, we divided motivation into negative and positive', Sid said.

'Negative motivation', Derek continued, 'is when we do something out of fear of punishment, or to get something unpleasant over with. Personally, I think negative motivation is very effective, and we don't use it often enough in training . . .'

'You can't say that! It's quite ridiculous,' Margaret said, interrupting.

'Yes, I think it's stupid to think that in this day and age such an approach is effective', Michael added.

'Well, I agree . . .'

'Just a moment', I said, interrupting Bob, 'Before we get into an argument about this, let's just listen to what Derek is saying, not from the point of view of whether or not we agree, but from the point of view of our own experience and whether negative motivation works for us or not. Go on Derek', I encouraged, 'and don't react to what the others have said.'

Derek continued and put forward some very interesting ideas for using negative motivation in conjunction with positive ideas. The group then discussed how they personally reacted when each of them was presented with the different forms of motivation. We prepared lists of motivational and demotivational attitudes and approaches, and there was general agreement that so-called negative approaches could be very effective.

In this example the intervention protected Derek's freedom to say what he wanted to say about motivation. Had the argument continued, Derek would have been defensive or aggressive, or he would have shut up. What happened was that the group allowed Derek the freedom to say what he believed, and from this the whole group moved forward.

Freedom of expression and behaviour is very important in signalling to the group that they can choose to be more fully themselves. This is very valuable in releasing ideas, attitudes and behaviour that people might not otherwise bring to the public arena for fear of being dismissed or ridiculed.

When a group is permitted some freedom, the diversity that emerges is astonishing, and the unique importance of each individual becomes more evident.[1]

There are five aspects of protecting freedom that I try to be aware of when I am facilitating a group. These five are part and parcel of the whole of the group interaction and cannot really be separated out solely under the activity of protecting freedom, but I have done so for clarity.

Choice is essential at all times. Everyone in the group needs to feel able to make choices all the time. Choices about whether to comment, whether to share, whether to take part in exercises, whether to be angry, to swear, to laugh, to cry, or whatever. They are encouraged to choose, not just to respond. If I suggest playing a game, they can agree or say no or make another suggestion. In other words, they always have the freedom to choose.

Time is handled quite differently by different people. When I discovered that I was constrained by time, and how I let time control what I did and when I did it, and that my attitude to time stopped me being free, I stopped wearing a watch and freed myself from being managed by time. Now I use time by being present now, because that is the only place where time exists. When working in groups, time should not be allowed to interfere with what is happening. The right time for anything is when we are ready, and not what it might say on a programme.

Of course, there is a requirement to respect the needs of others such as the people preparing meals, but we can work this into our thinking without letting time dominate what happens. Or as Kahlil Gibran puts it:

Of time you would make a stream upon whose bank you would sit and watch it flowing.[3]

On an individual level, people need time in the group to respond and the group should respect the time people need for reflection, or to construct what they want to say. Being able to take time is an important element in having freedom.

Space, both physical and psychological, is important in the group. If I don't feel that I have space to be myself, if I feel my boundaries are being invaded, then I become defensive and put up my protective shield. In such a state I am not free to choose, except to choose to withdraw, which benefits neither me nor the group. Of course, as a group member I need to express how I feel about my own space, so that everyone knows what I consider my boundaries are, and I need to let the group know as I make adjustments. This is true whether I am a group member or facilitator.

Tolerance is something that I have to work at. When I hear or see something I don't like, I can choose to tolerate what is happening or not. If I choose not to tolerate it I have to do something: either leave or stop it happening. If I choose to tolerate it, I do not have to agree with the statement or behaviour, or condone it, but I might learn something from being aware of what is happening, or even exploring it more fully. As a facilitator I need to be able to tolerate a great deal, including, sometimes, personal abuse and ridicule. If I cannot tolerate these things then I cannot learn what caused them to appear.

The *language* used in the group can have a limiting effect on freedom if it is full of 'musts' and 'shoulds' and 'must nots', and 'should nots'. If the group choose to set their own ground rules, then as the facilitator I feel I need to point out how this might limit choice and hence freedom, but not to prevent the group choosing how they want to be: they can always change later.

Freedom is, for me, an essential ingredient in the recipe for successful facilitation, which is why I am so keen to protect it within the group environment.

References

1. Bach, Richard (1978) *Illusions*, London: Pan.
2. Rogers, Carl R. (1983) *Freedom to Learn*, Columbus, Ohio: C.E. Merrill.
3. Gibran, Kahlil (1991) *The Prophet*, London: Mandarin.

20 Inviting participation

You are never given a wish without also being given the power to make it come true. You may have to work for it however.[1]

If I wish for things in the group to be a certain way, then I may have to act to influence how things are. If I am happy with how things are, then I have no need to act. In both these ways I am participating in the group being as it is.

Participation in a group should always be a matter of choice for the individuals in the group, but there are moments when people need to be invited to participate. Freedom (see previous chapter) includes being able to choose not to participate—or does it? Surely once we join a group, unless we withdraw completely, we are participating all the time.

But then perhaps there is a perception that participation means being active in 'doing' things. So there is a sense that if I choose not to join in a particular activity that I am not participating, even if I am still there. So what I mean, in the context of groups, is that if I am in attendance I am participating. This might imply that I never need to invite people to participate, but if as the facilitator I want to help the group to move forward I might well want to invite people to take part and share more fully in what the group are doing. They are participating by being there, but I might want to find ways for them to participate differently in the group activity. This desire for change in the way people are participating may also come from other members of the group who want to feel supported in some activity.

Derek, Greg and Melanie had been facilitating the group in a session about 'fun'. We had divided into three groups of four and each group had proceeded to devise a way of learning something about facilitation through a 'fun' activity. One group had decided to organize a treasure hunt, with the clues involving key points about facilitation. Another group had devised a crossword for the rest of us to do. And the group I was in had devised a short funny play about someone who attended the wrong course.

It was early evening and we were summarizing how to use fun as a key part of learning. We had written a list on the flip of the ways of using fun. Someone had written, 'Introducing fun, without being silly, is an important ingredient in training'. I had noticed that, though the various activities have been funny, they had been somewhat restrained.

'I have really enjoyed this afternoon', I said, 'and before we finish I would like someone to do something really silly'. Everyone laughed, and Bob said, 'Stretch your hands out in front of you. Keep them touching at the wrists and clap them together. Now say "Oink Oink Oink" '.

We all did this and we collapsed laughing. Then Greg got us to do something silly, and it became a sort of contest, and everyone had a go, with the activities becoming increasingly silly. Finally, we stopped laughing and headed for a pre-dinner drink. As I left the room I noticed someone had crossed out three words on the flip: 'without being silly'.

The way we participate and our willingness to join in has been largely conditioned by our past experiences, so that some of us are hesitant and others rush in. Facilitation is about making anything possible for the group and the individual members. So inviting people to participate can be an important way of enabling things to happen.

The strategy for dealing with group awareness is to first heighten, or make explicit what the concern is, and then to translate the awareness of the concern into excitement, then into action and interaction between group members.[2]

I use a variety of ways of inviting participation which once again follow a continuum from gentle to more purposeful.

Assuming that people will follow me or others in the group if we start doing something. Rather than state, 'Right now we are going to . . .' or 'I am now going to . . .', I prefer just to start doing it. I may stand and walk out, or write something on the flip chart, or ask a question, or whatever. By my action I will invite others in the group to follow. If I choose to follow someone else, by so doing I am inviting others to join me.

Christopher Robin was sitting outside his door putting on his big boots. As soon as he saw the big boots, Pooh knew that an adventure was going to happen, and he brushed the honey off his nose with the back of his paw, and spruced himself up as well as he could, so as to look Ready for Anything.[3]

Tempting people to join in nearly always works. There are two main ways to do this. The first is by curiosity. If I create a situation which engages their curiosity, people will almost always want to find a way of satisfying it. Secondly, I can tempt people by challenging them, either individually or as a group. Both curiosity and a challenge are almost irresistible ways of encouraging people to be more actively involved in what is happening.

By asking for *volunteers* I can generate a sense of challenge and fun, and often involve people who tend to be less active. When I ask for volunteers I nearly always do so without them having a clear idea of what I may be asking them to do. I can also use this approach to involve everyone in the group at some time or other during the workshop.

Asking people to do something is more direct, but very simple. They know that they can choose to decline my request, either as a group, or as individuals. The secret is only to ask when you are aware that people are holding back and just want a little encouragement, unless the intention is to challenge them. There are certain moments when I may not accept the first refusal I am given. On these occasions I may choose to try to persuade people to take part.

Persuasion should be exercised with care depending upon the people and situation. When I ask people to take part they may want to, but still decline. If I immediately accept this they may be disappointed and say, 'You didn't try very hard', in which case I can say, 'Well do you want to?', and I am into gentle persuasion. I can, of course, increase the degree of persuasion.

Sometimes, when I have suggested an activity to the group, one or other of the members may ask me what we are going to do it for. They are rarely satisfied with my usual answer, 'To see what happens'. Nor do they often believe that I don't know where something we are doing may lead. I find that many people have grown up with the strong message that, 'You have to do things for a reason'.

I am often challenged, especially in the early days of a group, for reasons for doing what we are doing. This challenging may be expressed as a need to know 'why' something is being done, or, 'What are we expected to learn from this?'.

When this happens I have a number of choices: to turn the question back; give a reason; ask for tolerance in going with it; suggest we will look at reasons after rather than before; get into explanations about process; or to discuss why they need a reason to do something. There are probably other options that I might consider, but I usually go for the last of those mentioned above.

Piglet thought that they ought to have a reason for going to see everybody, like looking for Small, or organizing an expotition if Pooh could think of something.

Pooh could.

'We'll go because it's Thursday,' he said, 'and we'll go to wish everybody a very happy Thursday. Come on Piglet.'[3]

References

1. Bach, Richard (1978) *Illusions*, London: Pan.
2. Zinker, Joseph (1978) *Creative Process in Gestalt Therapy*, London: Vintage.
3. Milne, A.A. (1986) *The Book of Pooh Quotations*, London: Methuen.

21 Releasing potential

You are led through your lifetime by the inner learning creature, the playful spiritual being that is your real self.

Don't turn away from possible futures before you're certain you don't have anything to learn from them.

You're always free to change your mind and choose a different future, or a different past.[1]

We all have the inherent ability or capacity, not yet realized, for growth, development and coming into being. This potential is hidden, suppressed and limited by past conditioning. When we examine our self-image we tend to find that it has been formulated by the information we have been given by others about ourselves: the art teacher who continually tells us we will never be a painter; the parent who tells us every day that we are too soft and sensitive; the bully who is praised by his bully father; and so on.

We tend to create our own barriers and boundaries that reflect what we have listened to for so long, and we come to believe that they are true. When we are offered the freedom and support of a well-facilitated group we get glimpses of this constrained potential and want to explore further. The facilitator has to be quick to spot this and to help people to reach for their potential.

Given this freedom and opportunity, most people will move towards growth and self-enhancement. However, this process is one of considerable risk and endeavour. People choosing this journey have to turn their backs on a history of doubt and negativity.

It would be grossly inaccurate to suppose that the organism operates smoothly in the direction of self-enhancement and growth. It would perhaps be more correct to say that the organism moves through struggle and pain towards enhancement and growth.[2]

It is not surprising then that when people get a glimpse of their potential they often hesitate to go further. 'No, I can't do that', or 'I've never been able to do that', or 'No, I don't have the hand–eye coordination to juggle'. I often put a sign up at my workshops which says:

If you can talk you can sing.
If you can walk you can dance.
Anyone can juggle and ride a
unicycle including you.
But you have to want to.

To assist people to release their potential, facilitators have to try to engender an environment which is safe (non-threatening), where people trust each other, where there is a common belief that what is to be attempted can be achieved, and where the effort is encouraged and supported. This also means a complete acceptance of mistakes and failed attempts that will inevitably lead to success. If people are not free to get it wrong then they won't attempt it, unless forced to try, which is not part of facilitation.

I have learned throughout my life as a composer chiefly through my mistakes and pursuits of false assumptions not by my exposure to founts of wisdom and knowledge.[3]

I believe that people can explore their potential by doing three things, described below.

The first is looking at *possibilities* rather than impossibilities. If you can look at anything that you want to do as possible, regardless of how you can do it, i.e. to separate the thought of it being possible from the action to make it possible, it does in reality become possible. Once we accept and believe something to be possible, then finding ways to make it happen becomes an option that never existed when we thought it to be impossible. This is the first and most vital step to reaching our potential.

On Thursday evening, after dinner, we decided to draw lots for who was to facilitate the evening session. I prepared some straws with one being shorter than the others. I thought it would be an interesting experiment to experience someone drawing the short straw. In the event it was Doreen. She was quite shocked.

'I just couldn't possibly do it', she said breathlessly, 'will someone else please do this evening?'

'Well, if you really don't want to, I . . .'

'Just a moment', I interrupted Sid, 'before someone takes over from Doreen, I would like to ask Doreen what is stopping you from facilitating the session?'

'I haven't got any experience,' she said.

'And?', I asked.

'And I'm frightened of taking the responsibility.'

'And?', I asked again.

'And I don't want to make a mess of it.'

'Do you think it could be possible for you to facilitate this evening?', I asked her.

'I suppose so', she answered.

'You don't sound convinced', I responded.

'No I'm not', she said.

'Could you close your eyes and just picture yourself facilitating the evening really well?', I asked her.

She closed her eyes and was quiet for a moment. Then she started to smile still with her eyes closed. 'What's happening now?', I asked her.

'It's going really well, and everyone is joining in.'

Then she opened her eyes and said, 'But that's only in my mind. Maybe it won't go as well in practice'.

'So what's the very worst that could happen?', I asked her.

'I could dry up and not know what to do next', she replied after a moment's thought.

'And if that happened, what options would you have?', I asked.

She thought for a moment and said laughing, 'To hand over to you, or to ask someone to help, or to ask the group what they wanted to do'.

'OK', I said, 'what do you want to do now?'

'I think I'd like to have a go.'

'Would you like anyone to assist or support you?', I asked her.

'Yes, Jennifer, if she's willing.'

'Of course I am', Jennifer said, without hesitation.

'So why don't you start then?', I suggested.

Doreen then proceeded to facilitate a very motivating and enjoyable evening on the 'training spectrum', which we all agreed had been excellent. As we finished, I asked Doreen, 'How do you feel now?'.

'Wonderful', she said, 'I just didn't know I had it in me.'

When we are unsure of ourselves it helps if we can *reach out* to an individual or the group to be with us. This is much harder to do than most of us ever admit. Asking for what we want from another person in a simple and direct way seems to have been knocked out of us in our childhood. Did you ever hear the expression, 'Those who ask don't get'? And did you ever experience the result of not asking, which was that you didn't get anyway?

What follows from this is a belief that we are undeserving, and so we hesitate from asking for what we want. So when we want help to take a step forward in our lives, we don't think anyone will respond, and worse, we don't even know how to ask.

Breaking through is the really hard thing to do. When we set up a barrier to our own activities it is harder to break down than any other externally created barrier. We set it up in the first place as a form of protection. It is like the castle wall, safe inside, but also preventing us from exploring outside, like a prison we choose for ourselves that has an open door, yet we spend our time looking out of the barred window at the world we can't enter.

The decision to break through our own barriers comes from within ourselves, from a belief that we can make it through to the other side. The facilitator is there to support us through this process, to encourage us to have a go, and to be there with us when we do it. Of course, in the 'artificial' world of the workshop, breaking through is quite different from how it is in our 'real' world, but it is a start, and it need not be a traumatic experience. It can be done through talking, singing, dancing, drawing, painting or any other way that seems appropriate at that moment.

On Friday morning we agreed to start a little later because of the party the night before which had started after Doreen's session and gone on for some time. But we were all there on time.

'Before we start anything else, I want to say something', Sid said. 'Last night, after the party, I was talking to Greg and I realized that I have spent a long time working in training, and instead of having 30 years' experience I have one year's experience repeated 30 times. Well, maybe not quite, but it feels like that, and what I want to do before I leave this workshop is to do a session in a way that is completely different from what I would normally do.'

The group were quiet for a moment. Sid was clearly nervous and his statement had taken a lot of effort.

'What do you want from the group Sid?', I asked him.

'Well, I would like the OK to facilitate the next session on leadership, and I would like Greg, Bob and Jennifer to help me.'

The group agreed to go along with Sid and the three people he asked agreed to help. Sid then asked his three helpers to join him in another room for a briefing. Meanwhile he asked the rest of the group to discuss in pairs what they liked and disliked about leaders. When they returned we divided into three groups. Sid joined one of the groups. Each group then discovered that it had a leader, or at least my group discovered it when Greg told us he was leading us, which he did very directively.

After about 40 minutes we reassembled in the main group and each group had to present its solution to dealing with a problem. What we discovered was that one of the groups, mine, had a directive leader, another elected their own leader once they knew the problem, and the third group operated without a designated leader.

We then went on to discuss what it was like being in our group and how it affected our ideas about what we liked and didn't like, and the effectiveness of the particular leadership approach. During all this, Sid stayed virtually silent, just making the occasional comment. Finally Sid asked for a volunteer to sum up the session, which Joe did.

'So how was that for you?', I asked Sid.

'It was the first time I have ever run, I mean facilitated, a session without leading from the front and by sharing responsibility for what we learned with the group.'

'And now you have done it very successfully, how do you feel?', I asked.

'Absolutely great! I feel pleased and excited and really good about myself', Sid said, with a lot of pleasure.

Releasing potential is possible if facilitators stay in touch with the group energy and the way that individuals interact within the group. But great care has to be taken to guide the process gently. It takes great courage, even in a safe and protective environment, to reach out, and/or break through to explore our potential. If we don't respect the feelings of the members of the group, and trust them to know when the time is right for them, we risk adding further layers of stone to the castle wall that they are safe behind.

'Piglet,' said Rabbit, taking out a pencil, and licking the end of it, 'you haven't any pluck.'

'It is hard to be brave,' said Piglet, sniffing slightly, 'when you're only a Very Small Animal.'[4]

References

1. Bach, Richard (1978) *Illusions*, London: Pan.
2. Rogers, Carl R. (1951) *Client Centred Therapy*, London: Constable.
3. Stravinsky, Igor (1966) *Themes and Episodes*.
4. Milne, A.A. (1986) *The Book of Pooh Quotations*, London: Methuen.

22 Empowering action

Argue for your limitations and sure enough they're yours.[1]

For me, the main aim of facilitation is to enable something to happen. What this action is will depend upon the situation, the subject and the people. The action may be a change in behaviour, a new approach to something, or a major life change. No matter how large or small the action, the facilitator should be able to help the individual, or group, to take the action, or to make a commitment to act.

Facilitation is not a process of causing or invoking change. It is a process of helping people to recognize that change is possible. To act for an individual or the group is disempowering, and is the exact opposite of what I believe facilitators should be doing. Yet there are times when people are struggling, so that the temptation to 'show them how' or to do it for them is almost too great to resist. It is exactly the process of struggling which leads to change.

It was late on Friday morning and we had been working on an exercise to simulate learning to ski. Jennifer was facilitating the session on 'simulation'. We had divided into three groups and each group had produced a skiing simulation. We had laughed a lot, and learned a lot about simulating, which we had written on a flip chart. The group was now sitting quietly waiting. Jennifer was looking nervous and unsure.

'What's happening now for you, Jenny?', I asked her.

'I'm stuck: I don't know what to do next', she answered.

'And how does it feel being stuck?', I asked.

'Awful. I feel nervous and embarrassed and stupid', she said.

'And what would you like to do about it?', I said.

'Run away, disappear, go and hide', she said, smiling.

'OK, that's three options', I said, 'now think of a few more.'

'Well, I could ask the group what to do next', she said, after a moment's thought. 'Or I could ask you. OK, I'll ask you: what should we do now?'

'Before I give you my ideas, tell me how you wanted this session to go when you prepared it', I said.

'Well, I wanted us to do the simulations, then produce the list of what we had learned and then discuss the different ways that we could use simulation in training', she answered.

'OK, so let's do that', I said.

'Do what?', she questioned, frowning.

'Discuss the different ways of using simulation, just as you suggested', I said.

'Of course', she said, 'I'd forgotten that part of my plan, thanks'.

And that is what we did to complete a very good session.

Empowering action can be done using a variety of ideas that include encouragement, support, doing things together, challenging and contradicting. The aim is to create an atmosphere where change becomes a desirable option, not from seeking any specific change, but from recognizing more fully where we are and where we want to be.

When a facilitator creates, even to a modest degree, a classroom climate characterised by all that she can achieve of realness, prizing, and empathy; when she trusts the constructive tendency of the individual and the group; then she discovers that she has inaugurated an educational revolution. Learning of a different quality, proceeding at a different pace, with a greater degree of pervasiveness, occurs. Feelings—positive, negative, confused—become a part of the classroom experience. Learning becomes life and a very vital life at that. The student is on the way, sometimes excitedly, sometimes reluctantly, to becoming a learning, changing being.[2]

Most people have a realistic and rational fear of change. I am not sure where this comes from, but some of it is certainly our past conditioning. When I was young I recall being adventurous, always doing outrageous things and getting into trouble. Perhaps I did it for attention, or out of boredom. The why doesn't matter, though; what matters is that I learned to enjoy new things and danger. I learned very early to search out change and how to enjoy it. For many people, the early experience was different and change meant risking failure, ridicule and even punishment. It became more comfortable to avoid change and to stay within the known parameters of life.

Not only death but change itself calls forth terror and makes some people restrict themselves to functioning in limiting but familiar settings. For these people, change of job, or significant people in their lives or their relationships with them, as when children grow up or parents get older, are exceedingly difficult transitions. I-am-what-I-am gets hardened into I-am-what-I-have-always-been-and-what-I-always-will-be.[3]

Avoidance, putting off action until some future time, is a wonderful way to deal with our need to feel comfortable, to remove the struggle from life, to avoid change. There are several well-known sayings and proverbs that support his age-old attitude to change, for instance, 'You can't teach an old dog new tricks', and 'The leopard does not change its spots'.

'I think not today, dear, another day.'
'Tomorrow?' said Roo hopefully.
'We'll see,' said Kanga.
'You're always seeing, and nothing ever   happens,' said Roo sadly.[4]

Of course, change for the sake of change is not recommended, though it can sometimes provide a new perspective that might lead to a more meaningful change. One of my simple approaches to ensuring a continuing change of perspective is to keep changing seats in the group so that we all spend time close to and opposite different people. Even such a simple form of change can be difficult for some people.

Making changes in attitude and behaviour is seen as the evidence that people have learned. Whether this is a justified view or not it is widely held to be so. But if we accept that the power to take action comes from within, then the degree to which this is judged to be possible and desirable must come from the individual. Each of us has to decide for ourselves to what extent we want to act to reflect our learning in our day-to-day lives.

After a very pleasant lunch by the pool we gathered for what was to be the last session before closing the workshop. There were still a few items left on the agenda to cover, and I suggested that we looked for a moment at the agenda and the note we had made at the beginning of our own personal objectives. After a few minutes I suggested that we should decide what we wanted to do with the time we had left before tea.

'The programme we prepared yesterday has worked well', Derek said, 'so why don't we complete it?'

'Yes we could do that', I answered. 'Any more ideas?'

'I'd like to talk about ways in which we can use what we've learned', Greg offered.

'And I want to hear what Joe has to say about time, and Trevor about problem people', Margaret said.

'What about David and Bob? They still have to talk about case studies and exercises', Derek said.

'OK, well, I'm going to suggest that we work in pairs', I said, 'and that we do three things. First that we look at one significant way in which we can use what we have learned, second that we describe a personal experience during the workshop that is most memorable, and third that we say something that we want to say to the group.'

There were no dissenting voices. Perhaps my directive approach shocked them into agreement and action. The result was a very powerful and generous expression of personal commitment and feeling. Each pair stood together supporting each other while they spoke. Many of the comments were emotionally charged and highly personal, and the group cheered and applauded each pair when they finished. When all the pairs had spoken, we stood in a group, held hands, and shared a moment of complete harmony. It seemed to me that this was a very good place at which to close the workshop.

Perhaps the final assessment of whether any training is of value can only come from the recipients. If a formal assessment of a workshop is needed, then I think that the basis for doing this, as set out in my book

The Business of Training, is as good as any. For me, the success or failure of facilitation is whether the individuals involved think they have grown in ways that they recognize.

If the purposes of the individual and the group are the organising core of the course; if the purposes of the individual are met if he finds significant learnings, resulting in self-enhancement, in the course; if the instructor's function is to facilitate such learnings; then there is but one person who is in a position to evaluate the degree to which the goal has been achieved, and that is the student himself. Self-evaluation appears to be the logical procedure for discovering those ways in which the experience has been a failure and those respects in which it has been meaningful and fruitful.[2]

Joe and I did share with the group our views about 'Timing' and 'Problem people' before we left, and here they are.

Timing: the only important times are the start and finish of the workshop. In between these, everything is flexible to suit the needs of the group.

Problem people: there are no problem people, only problem facilitators, who can't cope with energy and creativity.

I also shared with the group what I think is the essence of facilitation, which is a combination of *simplicity*, *honesty* and *vision*.

It is exceedingly important that one allow oneself to be surprised in daily life. That he not be habit-bound or jaded. That he always have a sense of wonder about his own life and the lives and words, gestures, and images of others. One must always be ready for surprises.[5]

References

1. Bach, Richard (1978) *Illusions*, London: Pan.
2. Rogers, Carl R. (1983) *Freedom to Learn*, Columbus, Ohio: C.E. Merrill.
3. Polster, E. and Polster, M. (1974) *Gestalt Therapy Integrated*, London: Vintage.
4. Milne, A.A. (1986) *The Book of Pooh Quotations*, London: Methuen.
5. Zinker, Joseph (1978) *Creative Process in Gestalt Therapy*, London: Vintage.

The final exercise—learning outcomes

This exercise can be completed in a variety of ways:

- Chapter by chapter
- as key learning takes place
- on completion of the book
- after a period of reflection
- in any other way you can think of

You might want to make lists, draw pictures, or use mind maps (see *The Business of Training*). Be as creative as possible.

This is not an exercise which can ever be complete, and much of the learning benefit of this book will only come when you practice the ideas it contains.

So here are two pages for your creative use.

This is what I have learned about facilitation

This is what I
will do with my
learning

Appendix 1: Introductions

Derek 'My name is Derek Weston. I am the Northern Region Training manager. I am 37 and I have been in training/education all my working life. When I got my degree I stayed on and did a masters degree and then I became a lecturer. I moved into training six years ago.'

I asked him to tell us something more personal about himself.

'I am married with two children, both at school, and I enjoy badminton, tennis and swimming.'

Margaret 'My name is Margaret, not Maggie. I am the regional coordinator. I enjoy working in training, but I have very little experience of running groups. I am engaged and I play hockey and I like swimming and surfing. Oh, and I have worked with Bob and Gregory.'

'How old are you Margaret?', I asked.

'Guess,' she responded.

'Well, I'd say about 23', I said.

'Close, I'm 25', she said, smiling.

David 'I'm David Trench, so most people dig me, boom boom! Well I thought I would get it in first. I'm a retired Navy Captain, and my last posting was as head of the navigation training centre. I have been retired two years and I am now working as the Peak Training Centre Manager. Married with a grown-up daughter and two grandchildren.'

'Do you enjoy your grandchildren?', I asked.

'Yes, they are wonderful, and I suppose I spoil them.'

'You must be in your fifties, I imagine', I said.

'Yes, I'm 52, but I feel a lot younger', he said, laughing.

Bob 'My name is Robert James, but please call me Bob. I am 28 and single. I play golf and I run. Oh! I work as a Training Consultant.'

I asked Bob what kind of running he did.

'Well, mostly marathons and half-marathons.'

'Are you any good?', I asked.

'Well, my best time for a marathon is three twenty six, which I suppose is not too bad', he replied.

Gregory   'Gregory Willis. I'm 30, married with three children. My job is Training Consultant, and I like reading and DIY.'

'Well you packed a lot into that sentence', I said. 'Do you enjoy the work you do as a training consultant?'

'Yes, I do', he replied.

'Tell us a bit about what you enjoy', I suggested.

'I really enjoy working with the client to analyse and design the training solution', he said.

'What about implementing solutions?', I said.

'Yes, well, that's OK, but I have some problems dealing with groups of trainees.'

Michael   'My name is Michael King, and I prefer Michael to Mike. I am the Southern Region Training manager. I'm 41 and I've been involved in personnel and training for 22 years—all with this company. I have a lot of experience with groups and I am looking forward to what we are going to learn from Trevor. I'm divorced and have two children who live with their mother. I play rugby and cricket.'

Trevor   'I'm Trevor. I have a varied career in business, but I have been a consultant in organizational change and personal development for 12 years. I am married with three adult sons. I read, write, play golf, ski, and I am a keen walker. I am also looking forward to what I am going to learn from everyone here, and to getting to know you all.'

'How old are you?' Margaret asked, getting her own back.

'Well, this time you can guess', I said.

'Well, it's hard to tell with the beard, but I would say between 48 and 53.'

'You're right', I said.

Jenny   'My name is Jennifer Smith, Jenny for short. I'm 26 and I work as a Training Consultant. I am also studying part-time for a masters degree in psychology. I have read your book Trevor.'

'Which one?', I asked.

'*The Business of Training*, I am looking forward to seeing how you work in practice. I am married, but no children yet. Oh! and I am 26 and a bit.'

Joe   'I'm Joe. I think I know, or have met, most people here. I am a Training Programme Designer and I have been on two of Trevor's workshops, and I am here to help him with this workshop, as well as to learn. I am single, and I enjoy windsurfing.'

Then Jenny said, 'Don't be shy Joe, tell us the rest'.

'Well, I am currently the Southern District windsurfing champion.'

'And how do you find time to enter all the competitions and practice?', I asked.

'I live by the beach, and I use my holidays, and I am allowed special leave for the important events', he said.

Doreen   'I'm the Training Administrator at Head Office. Oh! My name is Doreen Johnson. I'm not married and I play tennis and cycle.'

'You sound and look very nervous', I said.

'Yes, that's just how I feel', she said, with a nervous smile.

'Would you like to say some more about your nervousness', I encouraged.

'Well, I feel very young and inexperienced, and I'm not sure what to do', she answered.

'OK, well, perhaps from time to time you can tell us how you are feeling, because it's OK to feel and be exactly how you want to be on this workshop', I said.

Sid   'My name is Sydney Wellington, generally known to everyone as Sid. I'm the daddy here, being 59. I have worked in training for 30 years, and I am the Western Region Training manager. I am married and we have four children and six grandchildren. I enjoy gardening, sailing and golf.'

'I've come on the workshop with quite a lot of scepticism, and I think I have a lot to learn about facilitation, but I doubt if it's relevant to the work I do.'

'OK, thanks for the honesty. We'll have to wait and see', I said.

Melanie   'Well, isn't this all very interesting? I'm Melanie, people call me Mel for short, but I really don't like it. I've been working here for 6 years, and I'm now a training consultant. Outside work I spend a lot of time with an amateur dramatic group and we are rehearsing at present for *Hobson's Choice*. I'm single, well, separated from my husband, but I like to think of myself as single. We have no children, which I suppose is a blessing. I'm looking forward to the workshop and I expect that I'm going to learn a lot.'

Appendix 2: Agenda setting

The following are the individual comments of the group members after the agenda setting exercise.

David 'I've found the approach interesting. I didn't realize that there could be so many ideas about what we could learn. I think this agenda is much more extensive than one Trevor could have produced and I feel it's ours. I did at first think everything was very strange, but I'll stick with it.'

Bob 'I think it has been a very good approach. I've enjoyed it and I think we will do very well if we cover everything on the agenda.'

Gregory 'It has been hard for me to get involved because I'm not used to it, but I've enjoyed it, which surprises me. I feel involved and part of the group.'

Michael 'Yes, well this self-development approach is not new and it can be very effective. Like, I think what we have done is to produce a very good agenda, but then we do have a lot of experience in the group.'

Trevor 'Well, I've enjoyed the exercise, and doing it has helped me to get to know the group, and I think we have produced an agenda that I find exciting and challenging.'

Jenny 'I must admit that I have felt frustrated and irritated, but we have produced an agenda that I would never have produced on my own. I don't like the way that Trevor deflects questions back to the group. I find it irritating.'

Joe 'This is the third time I've done this exercise with Trevor and I think it's great. The group are involved, we have an excellent agenda, and I just love the way that everyone has a say, which is equally important.'

Doreen 'This is the first workshop of this kind that I have been on, and it has all been fascinating. I had no idea that we would be doing what we are doing. I thought it would be teaching and role play. I have enjoyed this different approach.'

Sid 'It's been great. I can't see myself doing this and it wouldn't be relevant for most of the training I do, but it's OK.'

Melanie 'I think it has been magic, the way that we have produced this agenda and begun to get to know each other. I have been on five-day workshops where I haven't had this much contact in the whole workshop. I like the way that Trevor just nudges us along and encourages us to do the work. I can't believe it's only Monday morning.'

Derek 'Well, I'm not sure. I have been feeling angry and frustrated that we haven't been working the way I am used to. I want to be given information and told what's happening, but we do seem to be working well as a group, and I admit that the agenda is way beyond what I would have thought. I will be surprised if we achieve even half of it.'

Margaret 'I don't know what to say. I agree with Melanie: it has been a revelation. I just wonder what else we're going to do that is so different. I like it.'

Appendix 3: People, process, content

In Chapter 3, the group agreed to an experiment which led to four groups making a short presentation to explain Figure 3.1 (see p. 12) and to suggest how the group as a whole might continue to decide on their personal needs from the workshop. This appendix indicates the main points presented by each group.

Group 1: Margaret, Derek, Doreen

Derek spoke on behalf of the group and started by saying that the diagram was an over-simplified view of a very complex situation that involved psychology and learning theory.

The main point, the group thought, was that it is essential for people to be fully aware of what they want to get out of any situation, and to understand the processes or techniques they can use to do this.

The relationship of the three circles, the person at the centre, the process and the content, depicts the boundaries that come betwen people and learning and that the role of the facilitator is to see that these boundaries are broken down.

The group felt that the best approach to defining our individual needs is to decide on the relevant content, then the process we want to use, and finally to consider the effects it would have on us personally.

Group 2: David, Bob, Jennifer

Jennifer reported back for the group.

'I want to start saying that we decided we would each comment on the diagram and then we would discuss it, and finally we would summarise our ideas and I would report back.

'We did have some disagreement, which I think I should explain first. David took quite a different view from Bob and I. He considered that the emphasis should be content, with the facilitator providing the processes that were appropriate for the people.

'Bob and I thought that the diagram was indicating that people were at the centre of what was happening and that it is the process they use that enables them to learn the content that interests them.

'Overall, we found that the very simple diagram helped us to focus on the issues about what we need, and we have all produced a list of personal objectives for the workshop.'

Group 3: Michael, Gregory, Joe

Michael reported back very briefly, saying, 'We basically liked the idea that such a simple diagram can encompass so much. In essence we felt that the diagram represented the levels of facilitation, the human level, the process level, and the content level, and that it is very important that we look first at ourselves and our needs, and then at the processes we are going to use to meet these needs, and finally the information we are going to collect to enhance our knowledge and so meet our needs.'

Group 4: Sid, Melanie, Trevor

Sid said that the group had been very useful and that Trevor had spent more time listening than talking, but had contributed some interesting ideas.

'On the whole, we see the diagram in two ways, one as a cone with the person as the top having to go through a process to get at the information they need (Figure A3.1).

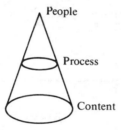

Figure A3.1   *People-orientated process*

'And second as a funnel with information having to be processed before it could reach the person (Figure A3.2).

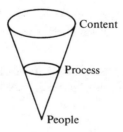

Figure A3.2   *Content-oriented process*

'From this we concluded that whichever direction we might choose to go in, the process is fundamental to us being successful in learning.'

Appendix 4: The Johari Window

The Johari Window was originally conceived by two psychologists, Joseph Luft and Harry Ingham, for their programme in group process. The window is a means of depicting the way we reveal ourselves to others and how others perceive us to be (Figure A4.1).

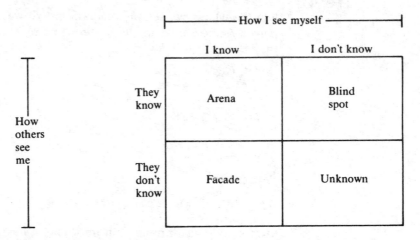

Figure A4.1   *The Johari Window*

The four panes of the window indicate the degree to which I reveal myself and the degree to which I am open to listen to and accept what others think about me.

If my window looks like Figure A4.2, it would indicate that I am very closed, revealing little and not listening; neither giving, nor taking in.

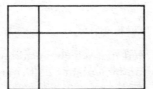

Figure A4.2   *Closed window*

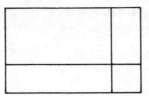

Figure A4.3   Open window

If my window looks like Figure A4.3, it could indicate that I am very open and revealing. I am willing to share myself. I am able to both give and receive information about myself.

If my window looks like Figure A4.4, then I could be willing to discover, i.e. take in, but not to give out; willing to learn about myself, but reveal little.

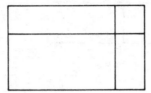

Figure A4.4   Learning window

If my window loooks like Figure A4.5, it could mean that I am willing to reveal myself, but not to hear what others think, and hence learn about myself.

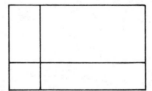

Figure A4.5   Revealing window

Of course, these are four extremes and any pattern could appear in-between those shown.

The *arena* pane represents what is in the public, or the group, domain. It is what we all know about me. I can choose to increase my arena by revealing more, and listening more to what people think about me.

The *blind spot* pane is reduced by my taking in more information about myself. When somebody says to me, 'You just don't see, do you?' I need to stop and think whether I have something to learn that can reduce my blind spot.

The *facade* pane represents what I hide from others. As I trust more, so I hide less, and of course once revealed it becomes part of my arena and can't be hidden away again. For many people, the provision of strict confidentiality is the only way they will remove their facade.

The *unknown* pane is that part of me I have not discovered and others don't see. It could be called the unconscious me.

What I think is important about the Johari Window is how it can help me to focus on my willingness, or lack of willingness, to share and grow as a person. It is likely that as I meet new people alone, or in groups I will gradually reveal more and extend my arena. So my window may start off in a new set of relationships as closed, and become increasingly open as time passes (Figure A4.6). It is the changing nature of what I see, what I want to see, and what I want others to see, which makes the Johari Window such a useful point of focus.

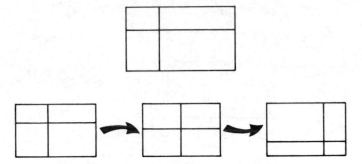

Figure A4.6   *Changing windows*

Appendix 5: A safe place for growth

I have stated repeatedly in this book that it is essential for the group to create its own environment for growth, with guidance from the facilitator if the group ask for it.

Some facilitators believe that it is useful to set or introduce ground rules for the group. I do not believe that facilitators can create a safe place for others to be. However, I do think that it is useful to be aware of what the elements that go to making a place safe might be.

I believe that the following are all important elements in creating a safe place.

1. The continuous application of the 'loving TOUCH' (see Chapter 4) which is based on;

   Trust for each other.
   Openness in attitudes and information.
   Understanding and acceptance of others.
   Confidentiality for what is learned about others.
   Honesty in sharing thoughts, feelings and emotions.

   The loving TOUCH cannot be forced on a group, but it can be brought to the group and modelled by the facilitator.

2. Ownership of, and responsibility for, thoughts, feelings, and emotions. Using language which indicates ownership such as 'I' instead of 'we', 'one', 'you' (see Chapter 9).
3. Attentive, concerned listening (see Chapter 8).
4. Using direct language, for example using statements instead of questions (see Chapter 9).
5. Addressing people directly using names, so that everyone knows who is involved in what you are saying.
6. Being prepared to share openly what you are experiencing about what is happening, and encouraging others to do likewise.
7. Respecting the time and space that other people need to express themselves fully, and making sure that other group members have this respect.

Index

Further titles in the McGraw-Hill Training Series